BAND SAW
BASICS

Gene & Mark Duginske

 Sterling Publishing Co., Inc.   New York

Metric Equivalents

INCHES TO MILLIMETRES AND CENTIMETRES

MM—millimetres   CM—centimetres

Inches	MM	CM	Inches	CM	Inches	CM
1/8	3	0.3	9	22.9	30	76.2
1/4	6	0.6	10	25.4	31	78.7
3/8	10	1.0	11	27.9	32	81.3
1/2	13	1.3	12	30.5	33	83.8
5/8	16	1.6	13	33.0	34	86.4
3/4	19	1.9	14	35.6	35	88.9
7/8	22	2.2	15	38.1	36	91.4
1	25	2.5	16	40.6	37	94.0
1 1/4	32	3.2	17	43.2	38	96.5
1 1/2	38	3.8	18	45.7	39	99.1
1 3/4	44	4.4	19	48.3	40	101.6
2	51	5.1	20	50.8	41	104.1
2 1/2	64	6.4	21	53.3	42	106.7
2	76	7.6	22	55.9	43	109.2
3 1/2	89	8.9	23	58.4	44	111.8
4	102	10.2	24	61.0	45	114.3
4 1/2	114	11.4	25	63.5	46	116.8
5	127	12.7	26	66.0	47	119.4
6	152	15.2	27	68.6	48	121.9
7	178	17.8	28	71.1	49	124.5
8	203	20.3	29	73.7	50	127.0

Library of Congress Cataloging-in-Publication Data

Duginske, Mark.
    Band saw basics / by Mark and Gene Duginske.
        p.   cm.
    Includes index.
    1. Band saws.   2. Woodwork.   I. Duginske, Gene.   II. Title.
    TT186.D83   1990
    684'.083—dc20   90-10127
                                                 CIP

Copyright © 1990 by Mark and Gene Duginske
Published by Sterling Publishing Company, Inc.
387 Park Avenue South, New York, NY 10016
Distributed in Canada by Sterling Publishing
% Canadian Manda Group, P.O. Box 920, Station U
Toronto, Ontario, Canada M8Z 5P9
Distributed in Great Britain and Europe by Cassell PLC
Villiers House, 41/47 Strand, London WC2N 5JE, England
Distributed in Australia by Capricorn Ltd.
P.O. Box 665, Lane Cove, NSW 2066
Manufactured in the United States of America
All rights reserved
Sterling ISBN 0-8069-7210-6

Contents

Dedication

This book is dedicated to our inventive friend,
Ed Morris.

Acknowledgments

We would like to thank our parents, who have always supported our creative endeavors, and our wives, Kate Morris and Mary Duginske, for their help and support. Also a note of appreciation to Chris Morris and Mary Duginske, who did most of the drawings, and Pat and Patricia Spielman, who contributed others. We would also like to thank the following people for their assistance: Charles Nurnberg, Barbara Reifschneider, David Morris, Garry Chinn, Peter Segal, Joni Lew, Stuart Braunstein, Frank Gorski, Brad Witt, Bill Stankus, Beau Lowerr, Toshio Odate, and the late Bill Rogers for his support and generosity. Finally, a note of thanks to Mike Cea, for his work in editing this book.

INTRODUCTION

The most effective way of doing woodworking is with power tools. Power tools offer speed and accuracy that is difficult to achieve with hand tools unless you have years of experience.

One power tool that is extremely popular is the band saw. There are several reasons for this. First, the band saw is very easy to use. In fact, some liken it to a sewing machine. It has a very simple design, and just a few working parts. The flexible blade (sometimes called a band) has cutting teeth on one edge. It is held under tension—that is, held taut—by two wheels. As the wheels rotate, the blade also rotates and cuts through the wood.

Second, the band saw is very versatile. There are two basic cuts that can be made in wood: straight and curved. The band saw can make both, in thick and thin wood. And, small band-saw blades have been recently developed that greatly increase the capability of the band saw to do intricate scroll work; this will further expand its use in the workshop.

Last, the band saw is probably the safest of all the power tools. It is certainly much safer than the table or radial arm saw. The blade is easily covered by the guard (a safety device that protects the operator from the saw), cuts at a relatively slow rate of speed, and applies a force directly towards the table that literally holds the wood down as it cuts, so that kickbacks are nonexistent. Kickbacks occur when the workpiece—the piece being cut—becomes pinched and the work is propelled at the person using the saw. Kickback is the major cause of table and radial arm saw accidents. Also, the band saw is quiet, which is an important but often overlooked factor.

When one considers all these points, it is easy to understand why the band saw is considered by many to be the ideal power tool for the beginning woodworker.

This book is geared towards anyone who has a

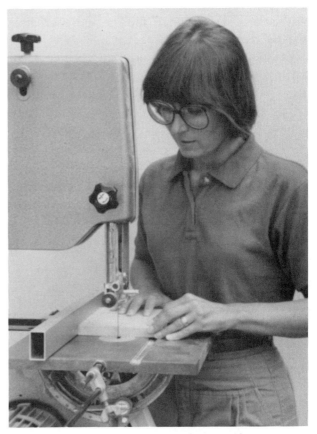

The band saw is a versatile and very safe power tool.

band saw or is considering buying one, but is unfamiliar with the tool. It explains how the band saw works, and how it can be used to its best advantage. It covers all the fundamentals: each part of the tool; how to determine which blade to use; how to maintain and safely use the tool; and proper sawing procedures. Then it gives a step-by-step account of all the techniques that have to be mastered to prepare the tool for use. These include adjusting the blade, thrust bearings and guides, and aligning the wheels. These techniques are simple and can be easily learned. They are also vital to getting the best possible use out of the tool.

The band saw can be used to make a variety of

cuts, and the techniques for these are explored and illustrated. This includes, to name just a few, scroll-sawing; using patterns and templates; making curves, circles, and straight cuts; and stack sawing. Other skills, like table-tilting cuts, sawing multicolored layers, kerfing, and using laminations are included for the more creative woodworker. In some cases, we show how to use jigs to facilitate these techniques. (Jigs are aids or fixtures which help you make the cut more easily.) Finally, the last chapter contains many projects on which you can test and develop your skills.

By following the principles and advice outlined in the following pages, the beginning woodworker will soon become a skilled band saw user. In time, he or she will discover that the band saw is the one tool in the workshop that is being used more and more frequently.

Chapter I

EXPLORING THE BAND SAW

The band saw is generally defined as a saw in the form of an endless steel band that runs over pulleys. The word endless means that the blade revolves in a continuous cutting motion.

The band saw was patented in 1808 by William Newberry of England. However, because the blades broke easily, the saw was not practical to use until 1846, when a Frenchwoman discovered a way to weld or unite newly developed spring steel. This discovery led to the creation of the first usable blade.

The band saw today is one of the most frequently used power tools in the workshop. Though it is used most effectively on wood, it can be used to cut other material, like steel.

How the Band Saw Works

The band saw is named after the type of blade that is used on the saw. (Blades, or bands, are discussed more fully in the next chapter.) This blade is a continuous metal band with teeth on one side. (See Illus. 1-2.) It is suspended over two or three metal wheels. As the wheels rotate, so does the band. This creates the sawing action.

Because the direction of the blade is always downward, there is no danger that the wood will be thrown at the operator. (See Illus. 1-3.) This is called kickback. There is always a danger of kickback when a circular saw is being used. For safety reasons, many woodworkers prefer the band saw, especially when cutting small pieces.

The unique feature of the band saw is that the workpiece can be rotated around the blade, creating a curve. (See Illus. 1-4.) It is the tool most often used when curves have to be cut in wood. But the band saw can also be used to cut straight.

Because the band-saw blade is fairly thin, it can cut thick stock with a minimum of horsepower. For this reason, the band saw is also often used when thick pieces of wood have to be cut.

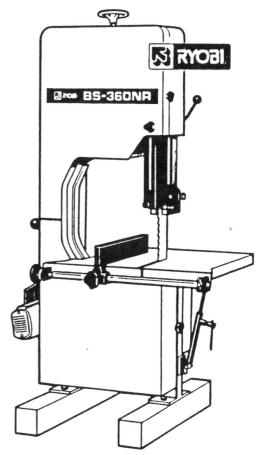

Illus. 1-1. *The band saw is a saw in the form of an endless steel band that runs over pulleys.*

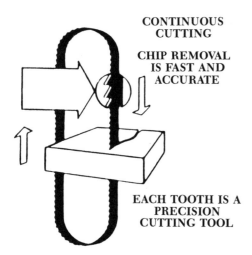

CONTINUOUS CUTTING

CHIP REMOVAL IS FAST AND ACCURATE

EACH TOOTH IS A PRECISION CUTTING TOOL

Illus. 1-2. *The blade used on a band saw is a continuous metal band with teeth on one side.*

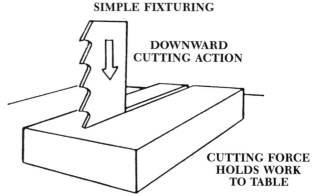

SIMPLE FIXTURING

DOWNWARD CUTTING ACTION

CUTTING FORCE HOLDS WORK TO TABLE

Illus. 1-3. *The band saw is considered a safe tool to use because the blade has a downward cutting motion. This prevents kickbacks, which is when the piece of wood being cut is thrown back at the operator.*

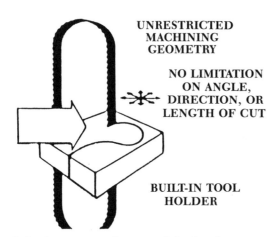

UNRESTRICTED MACHINING GEOMETRY

NO LIMITATION ON ANGLE, DIRECTION, OR LENGTH OF CUT

BUILT-IN TOOL HOLDER

Illus. 1-4. *One unique feature of the band saw is that the workpiece can be rotated around the blade, creating a curve.*

Parts of the Band Saw

The band saw does not have many parts, but you should be familiar with each one. Each part is discussed under the following titles, and is shown in Illus. 1-6.

Wheels

The blade is suspended over the two wheels (see Illus. 1-5). As the wheels rotate, the toothed

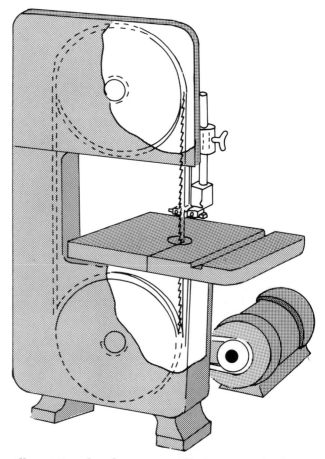

Illus. 1-5. *A band saw generally has two wheels. The bottom wheel powers the blade and pulls it downwards through the workpiece. The upper wheel is used to track and tension the blade. Tracking and tensioning are explored in Chapter 3.*

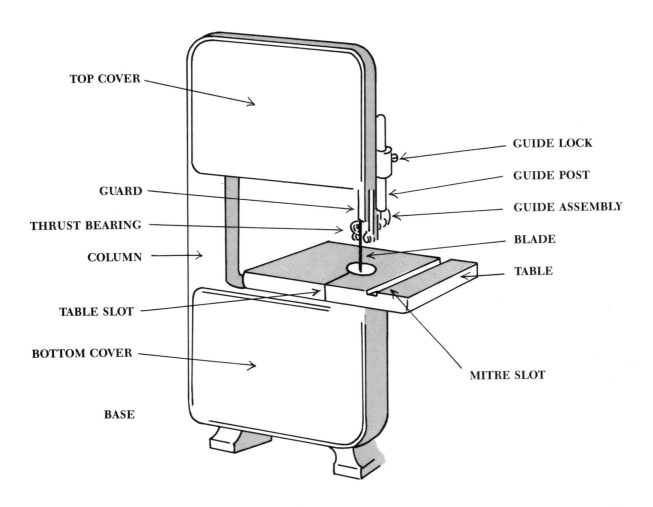

TOP COVER

GUIDE LOCK

GUIDE POST

GUARD

GUIDE ASSEMBLY

THRUST BEARING

BLADE

COLUMN

TABLE

TABLE SLOT

BOTTOM COVER

MITRE SLOT

BASE

Illus. 1-6. *Shown here is a typical band saw and the generally accepted terms used to describe its differ-* *ent parts. These terms sometimes vary. For example, the column is often called a post.*

blade also rotates, creating the downward cutting action. The wheels are usually covered with a piece of rubber called a tire. The tire cushions the blade and protects the teeth from contact with the metal wheel.

The bottom wheel is the drive wheel. It is attached to the power source either directly or through a belt. The bottom wheel powers the blade and pulls it downwards through the workpiece.

The top wheel has two functions, and is adjustable for each one. One function is balancing or tracking the blade on the wheels. The top wheel has an adjustable tilt mechanism that is used to

balance the blade.. The other function is to tension the blade. The wheel moves up and down. These functions are described in Chapter 3.

Frame

Most of the important parts of the band saw—including the wheels and table—attach to the frame. There are various styles of frame, and each manufacturer makes the frame differently.

Frames are either one-piece castings or of the skeletal type. One-piece castings are one large casting that provides both the main framework

Illus. 1-7. *This modern Sears band saw has a one-piece casting. This casting provides both the main framework and the cover for the back of the wheels.*

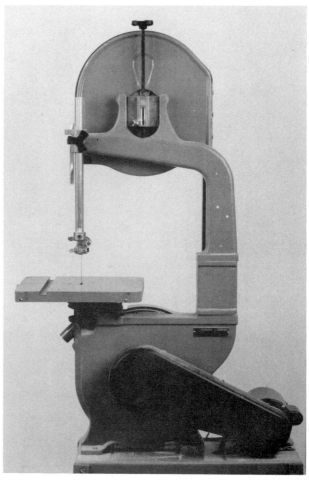

Illus. 1-8. *This Delta 14-inch (14-inch throat capacity) band saw has a skeletal framework and wheel covers. The wheel covers are attached for safety.*

and the cover for the back of the wheels. (See Illus. 1-7.) Skeletal frames are simply frameworks that are either cast or welded. A separate piece of sheet metal is attached to the frame to safely cover the back of the saw. (See Illus. 1-8.) This protective cover is called a wheel housing.

Cover

Covers protect the operator from the wheels and the blade. If the blade breaks, the pieces of blade are contained by the covers.

The covers are either of one or two pieces: Some are hinged (Illus. 1-9); some are attached with knobs or clips. The two most common materials used for covers are plastic and metal. Plastic is quieter and less susceptible to vibration.

Table

The workpiece rests on the table as it is fed into the blade. The table surrounds the blade. A large hole in the middle of the table around the blade allows the operator to make adjustments below the table. This hole is covered by the throat plate. (See Illus. 1-10.) The throat plate is made of either plastic or metal. A plastic plate is quieter and won't cause any damage if the blade accidentally touches it.

Table Slot A slot in the table allows the blade entry into the middle of the table. There is usually a mechanism to keep the two separated halves of the table in line with each other. (See Illus. 1-11). It may be a bolt, a pin, or a screw.

Illus. 1-9. *Some band saws have hinged covers. Hinged covers allow easy access to the inside of the band saw. This band saw has a two-piece hinged cover. (Photo courtesy of Delta)*

Illus. 1-10. *The parts of a typical band-saw table.*

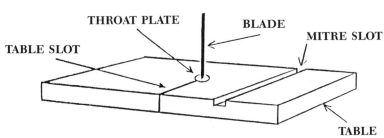

THROAT PLATE
BLADE
MITRE SLOT
TABLE SLOT
TABLE

Illus. 1-11. *Band saws have a mechanism for aligning the table on each side of the slot. Shown here is a level pin. The pin is gently tapped into the hole, forcing the two sides into proper alignment. To remove the pin, turn it with a wrench.*

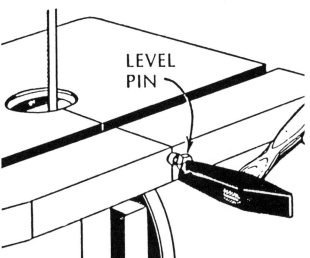

LEVEL PIN

Some manufacturers use the front rail. Make sure that you align the saw table halves. If you are negligent, you risk the chance of the two halves warping in opposite directions, causing an uneven table.

Table Tilt The table on most band saws is designed to tilt, which means that it can make bevelled or angled cuts. The table tilts away from the column up to 45 degrees. (See Illus. 1-12 and 1-13.) On some models, it also tilts towards the

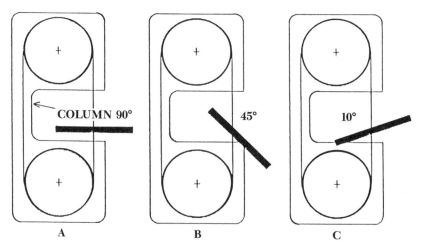

Illus. 1-12. *The band-saw table tilts away from the column up to 45 degrees. On some saws, it also tilts towards the column up to 10 degrees.*

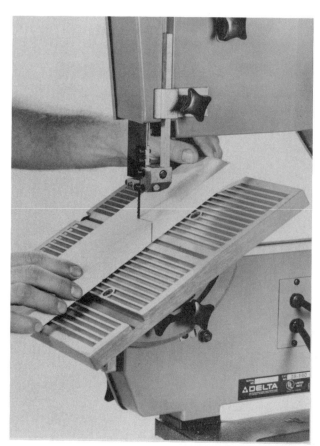

Illus. 1-13. *The tilted table allows the operator to make a variety of angled or bevelled cuts.*

Illus. 1-14. *This new Sears band saw has a tilting head. It is similar to the bevel band saws made in the past. This machine has a digital readout that indicates the bevel angle, blade tension, and blade speed.*

column up to 10 degrees. (See Illus. 1-12C.) This added feature may be handy at times, but it is not a necessity. Underneath the table there is an adjustable bolt or screw to help level the table back to 90 degrees after the table has been tilted.

Recently, Sears has started selling a band saw that has a stationary table and a tilting head. (See Illus. 1-14.) This was a common design on past band saws.

Trunnions The table is attached to two semicircular metal pieces called trunnions. (See Illus.

1-15.) The trunnion mates with another semicircular piece attached to the bottom of the table. This mechanism allows the table to angle. After the table is adjusted to the desired angle, it is locked in place with the trunnion lock. A scale and a pointer register the angle of tilt. The pointer and the levelling bolt should be adjusted to an accurate 90 degrees. The best way to do this is to use an accurate square. (See Illus. 1-16.)

Mitre Gauge Slot Most saws have a mitre gauge slot. (See Illus. 1-16.) This slot runs parallel to the

Illus. 1-15. *Shown here is the front trunnion on a band saw. Clean and lubricate the trunnion often if you are tilting the table frequently. Avoid grease as a lubricant because it traps sawdust. A lubricant such as Teflon works well.*

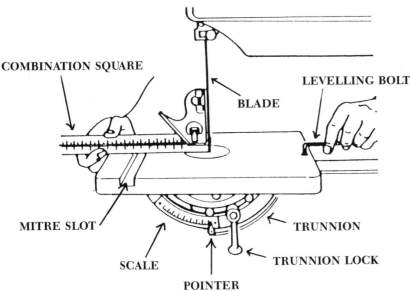

Illus. 1-16. *Shown here are the top and bottom of the band-saw table. Check the blade and table often to make sure that they are square.*

blade and accepts the mitre gauge bar, which is usually used for crosscutting (cutting across the grain of wood). The mitre gauge slot is very useful for owner-built jigs. Many jigs are designed to operate parallel to the blade, and the mitre gauge slot provides the most logical path.

Guide Assembly There are two guide assemblies, one below the table and one above the table. The top assembly is attached to a metal rod called the guide post. The whole upper guide assembly is adjustable up and down. (See Illus. 1-17.) The guide-post lock screw locks the post at the desired height. The blade guard is attached to the front of the guide post.

Each guide assembly consists of two guide blocks that are located on each side of the blade. The blocks hold the side of the blade in position. Each assembly also houses the thrust bearing, which keeps the blade from being pushed rearwards when the saw is cutting. (See Illus. 1-18.)

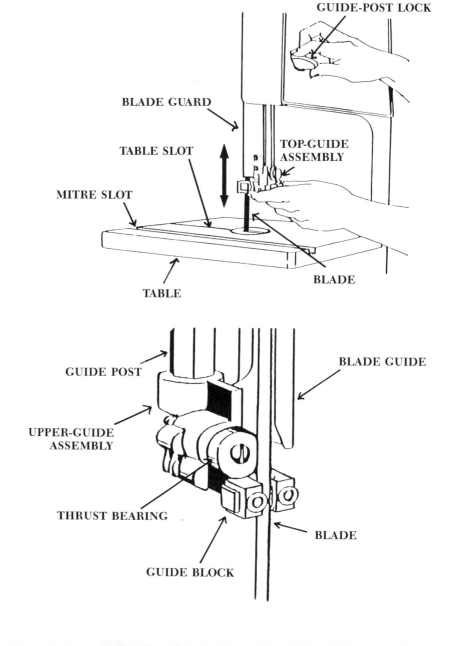

Illus. 1-17. *The upper guide assembly is adjustable up and down. The blade guard is attached to the front of the assembly. (A blade guard protects the operator from the blade.) For safety and performance reasons, lock the assembly approximately ¼ inch above the workpiece.*

Illus. 1-18. *A close-up of the upper guide assembly.*

Switch

You can turn the band-saw motor on and off with a switch. On some models, the switch is attached to the saw. On other models, it is on the stand.

There are safety devices designed on some switches. The Sears band saw, for example, has a removable plastic key. (See Illus. 1-19.) Unauthorized use of the saw cannot take place unless the plastic key is used.

If children may be tempted to turn on the band saw, make sure that you use some kind of protection. A locked electrical panel box protects the entire shop.

General Classifications

Though band saws come in many different styles, they are generally classified according to the widths of their throats. This is the distance between the blade and the column or post. (See Illus. 1-20.) For example, a band saw described as a 16-inch band saw has a throat width of 16 inches.

Band saws come with either two or three wheels. The number of wheels a band saw has determines the throat width of the tool. Band saws with three wheels have a large throat width. (See Illus. 1-21.)

Sometimes band saws are classified according to their "depth-of-cut" capacities. This refers to the thickest cut the saw can make. This distance is usually about 6 inches on consumer-grade saws. (See Illus. 1-22.)

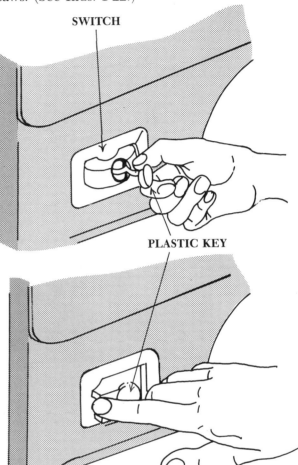

Illus. 1-19. *This switch—which is used on a number of Sears band saws—functions as a safety device. It will not operate until the plastic key is in place.*

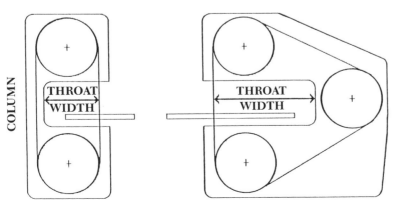

TWO WHEEL   **THREE WHEEL**

Illus. 1-20. *Band saws are usually classified according to the width of their throats, which is the distance between the blade and the column or post. Note that the band saw on the right, which has three wheels, has a wider throat capacity than the two-wheel band saw on the left.*

Illus. 1-21. *Shown here is one of the popular small band saws now available. It has a three-wheel design that allows for a wide throat capacity.*

Illus. 1-22. *The depth of cut refers to the thickest cut the saw can make.*

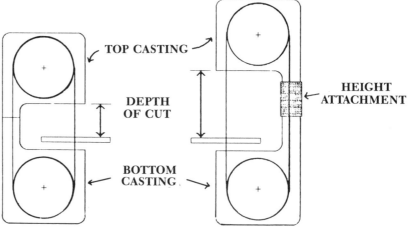

TOP CASTING

DEPTH OF CUT

HEIGHT ATTACHMENT

BOTTOM CASTING

Chapter 2

BLADES

Though band-saw blades all have the same basic design, they each have their own particular cutting characteristics. To get the best possible use out of a band saw, you have to use the blade that has the characteristics best suited for the given task. This can only be accomplished if you understand the different types of blade and their cutting characteristics.

Before exploring the general types of band-saw blade available, you should familiarize yourself with the terms used to describe them. Read the following table carefully. Refer to Illus. 2-1 while reading these terms.

Back   The back of the blade contacts the thrust bearing during the sawing process. Sometimes the back of the blade is hardened. This is best for cutting metal, which requires heavy feed pressure.

Body   The band material without the teeth. The body of the blade bends easily enough to tolerate the constant flexing cycle.

Body Width   The width of the blade minus the width of the gullet. Body width is the functional width of the blade, and determines the blade's beam strength (its ability to resist deflection).

Gauge   A term that refers to the thickness of the band.

Gullet   The space between the teeth that holds the sawdust during the cutting process.

Gullet Corner   The corner of the gullet. The sharper the corner, the greater the likelihood that the blade will break prematurely. Gullet corners are usually rounded for this reason. Blades usually break at the gullet corner.

Gullet Depth   The distance from the point of the tooth to the back of the gullet. The greater the depth, the greater the blade's capacity to hold sawdust.

Kerf   The width of the saw cut.

Pitch   A term used to describe how many teeth there are per inch of blade. It is usually referred to as Teeth Per Inch (TPI).

Rake Angle   The angle of the tooth face in relationship to the tooth back.

Set   The bend of the teeth. Set is measured at the widest point of the blade. The more set the blade has, the wider the kerf it cuts. With its teeth set, a blade cuts a curve wider than the body of the blade.

Side Clearance   The difference between the body of the blade and the kerf. Side clearance is determined by how the blade is set. It prevents binding in the kerf, and allows the workpiece to be rotated around a blade, creating a curve.

Teeth   The points on the blade that do the actual cutting on the table. The teeth on some blades are hardened.

Tooth Point   The cutting or scraping edge. The point does the most work and suffers the most wear during the sawing process.

Tooth Spacing   A term used to describe how far apart the teeth are. "Fine" refers to a blade with many teeth. "Coarse" refers to a blade with few teeth.

TPI   Teeth per inch.

Width   The distance from the front to the back of the blade. The wider the blade, the greater its beam strength.

Table One. *A clarification of the terms used to describe band-saw blades.*

Illus. 2-1. *Become familiar with the different parts of the blade.*

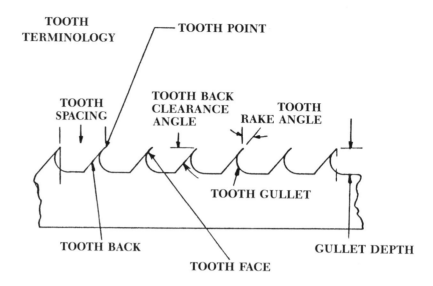

Factors That Determine Blade Performance

Two factors affect how a blade cuts. They are the width of the blade, and its pitch. Both are examined below.

Blade Width

Blades are usually classified according to their width, which is the measurement from the back of the blade to the front of the teeth. The width of the blade determines how tight a turn the blade can make. The *narrower* the blade, the *tighter* the turn. (See Illus. 2-2.) The *wider* the blade, the more likely it is to resist deflection. For this reason, wider blades are preferred over narrow blades when straight cuts are being made.

A ½-inch blade is the widest blade that is practical to use on a consumer-grade band saw. Some owners' manuals say that you can use a ¾-inch blade, but do not use a blade this wide on a saw that has wheels less than 18 inches in diameter. A ¼-inch blade is the most frequently used blade for general-purpose work. (See Illus. 2-3.)

For years, the smallest blade that was available was the ⅛-inch blade. This blade will make a

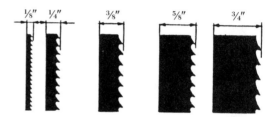

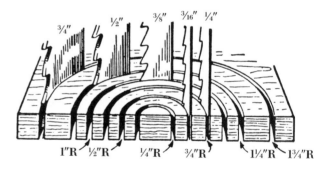

TURNING RADII OF BLADES

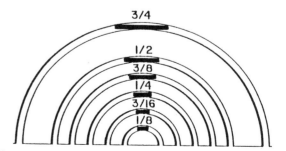

Illus. 2-2. *Narrow blades can cut tighter turns than wide blades.*

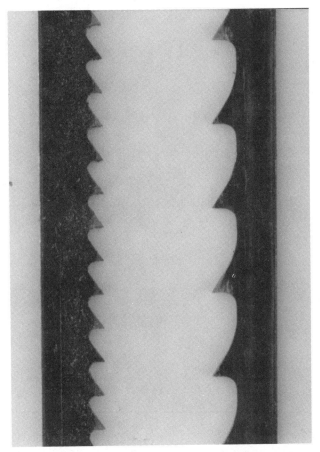

Illus. 2-3. One-quarter-inch blades are the most frequently used blades for general-purpose work.

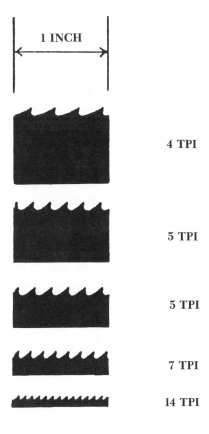

1 INCH

4 TPI

5 TPI

5 TPI

7 TPI

14 TPI

TEETH PER INCH (TPI)

Illus. 2-4. It is common for wide blades to have fewer teeth. When a blade does not have many teeth, it is referred to as coarse. Narrow blades often have many teeth. A blade that has many teeth is referred to as fine.

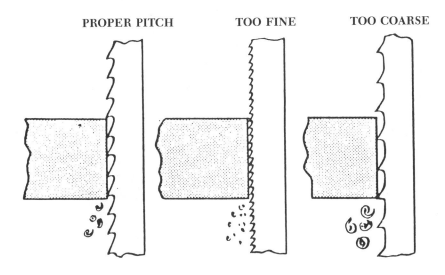

PROPER PITCH   TOO FINE   TOO COARSE

Illus. 2-5. The most efficient cut is made with a blade that has the proper pitch.

turn about the size of a pencil eraser. However, $\frac{1}{16}$-inch blades have recently been developed. A $\frac{1}{16}$-inch blade will make a 90-degree turn. This very small blade requires special nonmetal guide blocks, called "Cool Blocks." Cutting with this blade is discussed more fully in Chapter 7.

Pitch (Tooth Size)

The word pitch refers to the size of the tooth. The pitch is usually given in a number that refers to how many teeth are in one inch of blade (called "teeth per inch"). (See Illus. 2-4.) The words "coarse" and "fine" are used to describe the number of teeth in a blade. A coarse blade has few teeth. A fine blade has many teeth. The coarser the blade, the faster the cut.

It is important that you match the pitch of the blade to the material that is being cut. There should be at least three teeth in the material at any given time during the saw cut. A blade with more teeth will give a smoother cut, but one with too many teeth will create other problems, such as excessive heat and slow cutting. (See Illus. 2-5.) Excessive heat shortens the life of the blade because it causes the teeth to dull quickly. It also shortens the life of the band. There are certain things that indicate if a blade has the proper pitch, too fine a pitch, or too coarse a pitch. They are listed below.

Proper Pitch
1. The blade cuts quickly.

2. A minimum amount of heat is created when the blade cuts.

3. Minimum feeding pressure is required.

4. Minimum horsepower is required.

5. The blade makes quality cuts for a long period.

Pitch That Is Too Fine
1. The blade cuts slowly.

2. There is excessive heat, which causes premature blade breakage.

3. Unnecessarily high feeding pressure is required.

4. Unnecessarily high horsepower is required.

5. The blade wears excessively.

Pitch That Is Too Coarse
1. The blade has a short cutting life.

2. The teeth wear excessively.

3. The band saw vibrates.

Material Hardness When choosing the blade with the proper pitch, one factor you should consider is the hardness of the material that is being cut. (See Illus. 2-6.) The harder the material, the finer the pitch that is required. For example, exotic hard woods such as ebony and rosewood require blades with a finer pitch than American hard woods such as oak or maple. Soft wood such as pine is best cut with a blade that is fairly coarse. If the blade has too many teeth, the pitch in the pine will quickly clog the blade, decreasing its ability to cut.

HARDNESS AND PITCH

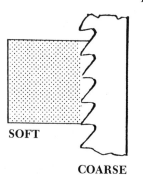
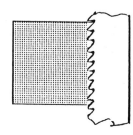
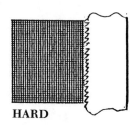

Illus. 2-6. *Hard material requires a blade with a finer pitch.*

SOFT

COARSE

HARD

FINE

Blade Teeth Characteristics

Two factors that indicate how a band-saw blade will cut are the set and form of the teeth. Both factors are examined below.

Tooth Form

The teeth on a blade come in one of two shapes. The face of the tooth is either 90 degrees to the body of the blade, which is called a 0-degree rake, or it has a slight positive angle, in which case it is called a hook tooth. (See Illus. 2-7.)

A blade with 0-degree rake cuts with a scraping action. This makes a smooth cut, but increases the heat caused by the cutting. A blade with hook teeth cuts more aggressively. It makes a rougher cut, but less heat is generated, which means that the blade can be used for a longer period of time.

Blades can be broken down into three general groups according to the form of their teeth.

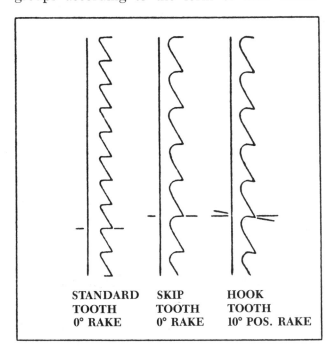

STANDARD TOOTH 0° RAKE   SKIP TOOTH 0° RAKE   HOOK TOOTH 10° POS. RAKE

Illus. **2-7.** *A blade with standard or skip teeth has a 0-degree-rake angle. A blade with hook teeth has a positive angle, which is usually 10 degrees.*

These blades are called standard-tooth blades, skip-tooth blades, and hook-tooth blades. They are discussed below.

Standard-Tooth Blades A blade with standard teeth has teeth spaced closely together. It has a 0-degree rake. This blade makes a smooth cut. It is especially useful for cutting small details and for cutting across (against) the grain of the wood, because it doesn't tear the wood as it cuts. It is the best blade to use when smoothness is a consideration. When cutting thick stock with a standard-tooth blade, make sure that you feed the stock slowly.

Skip-Tooth Blades The teeth on skip-tooth blades have a 0-degree rake, like those on standard-tooth blades, but every other tooth is removed. Thus, this blade has only half as many teeth. Because a skip-tooth blade is coarse, it cuts much faster, especially when the blade is used to cut with the grain.

A skip-tooth blade is best suited for cutting long, gentle curves. Although it doesn't cut against the grain as well as the standard-tooth blade or rip as well as the hook-tooth blade, it is often the most widely used blade because it provides the best compromise.

Hook-Tooth Blades The hook-tooth blade is the most aggressive blade. This is because it has a positive rake angle and the fewest number of teeth. It is particularly efficient at cutting thick stock, with the grain. This makes it the best choice for ripping and resawing. (See Illus. 2-8.) Ripping is cutting along the grain of the wood. Resawing is cutting a board in half through its width.

Tooth Set

The teeth on the band saw are bent or "set" sideways. Thus, the saw kerf (cut) is wider than the body of the blade. Set makes it easier for the band-saw operator to rotate the workpiece around the blade when creating a curved cut.

Illus. 2-8. *This hook-tooth blade is cutting red oak. It has a pitch of 3 teeth per inch. This pitch is best for cutting thick stock.*

The side clearance of the blade created by the set of the teeth also serves to decrease the friction between the blade and the workpiece on straight cuts. There are three basic set styles, as follow:

RAKER SET

WAVY SET

ALTERNATE SET

SET STYLES

Illus. 2-9. *Shown here are the three most common set styles for blade teeth. Some raker sets have every fifth or seventh tooth as the raker.*

Alternate Set Alternate-set teeth are set so that every other tooth is bent in the same direction. A blade with alternate-set teeth gives the most cuts

per inch, and thus gives the smoothest cut. Standard-tooth blades usually have teeth with alternate set. This type of blade is well suited to crosscutting (cutting against the grain of wood).

Raker Set Raker-set teeth are similar to alternate-set teeth except that some of the teeth, called rakers, are not set, or bent. Rakers clean the middle of the cut, and are used most often on skip- and hook-tooth blades. The design increases the efficiency of the cutting action but decreases the smoothness of the cut, because fewer teeth are cutting the side of the kerf.

Wavy Set A blade that has teeth with a wavy set has groups of teeth that are alternately set in opposite directions. This type of set is also used on the hand-held hacksaw, and is designed for cutting metal.

Blade Classifications

Band-saw blades are usually classified in three different groups: small, medium, and large. (See Illus. 2-10.) This takes into account the width, tooth form, and pitch of the blade.

Small blades usually have standard (regular)

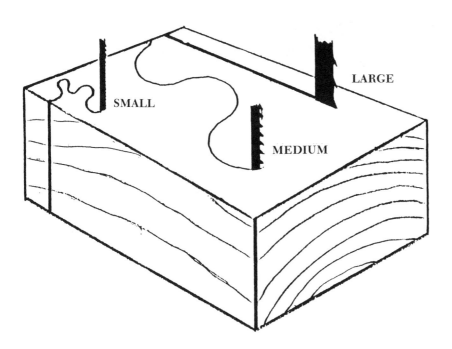

SMALL

MEDIUM

LARGE

Illus. 2-10. *Blades are usually divided into three groups: small, medium and large. The blade's width, tooth form, and pitch determine which group it belongs to.*

teeth and a fine pitch. Medium blades usually have skip teeth, with a raker set and a medium-to-coarse pitch. Large blades often have hook teeth, with a raker set and a coarse pitch. Not every blade can be so neatly classified, however. Consider the example of a ½-inch blade that has a pitch of 14 TPI (Teeth Per Inch) and standard teeth with an alternate set. This blade is large, yet its teeth are those that you would normally find on a blade classified as "small."

You can best prepare yourself by having at least one blade from each group. This way, you will be prepared for almost any situation.

The following chart gives descriptions of blades that fall into the three classifications.

	SMALL	MEDIUM	LARGE
WIDTH	¹⁄₁₆–⅛ inch	³⁄₁₆–⅜ inch	½ inch and over
PITCH	14–32 TPI (fine)	4–12 TPI	2–4 TPI (coarse)

Choosing a Blade

There are two primary factors to consider when choosing a blade. The first is the tightness of the curves that you are going to be cutting. This will determine the width of the blade. The second factor is the orientation of the grain that you are cutting. Both these factors are discussed here.

Blade Width

The width of the blade determines how tight a turn can be made. Until you become well acquainted with your saw, it is best to use the contour chart shown in Illus. 2-11 to determine which size blade to use for a specific application.

As an example, let's assume that you want to cut the number 2. You would need a ⅛-inch blade to cut the pattern because that corresponds to the tightest curve. With this blade, you can cut the curve in one uninterrupted saw cut.

There are other options, which would allow you to make this cut with a larger blade. These options will be discussed in detail in the next chapter.

You can also use everyday items such as coins or a pencil to determine which blade to use. A quarter is the size of the tightest cut that can be made with a ¼-inch blade. A dime is the size of the tightest curve that can be cut with a ³⁄₁₆-inch blade. A pencil eraser is the size of the tightest turn that you can make with a ⅛-inch blade.

Contour cutting: Blade width is determined by the smallest radius to be cut. Use this chart to find maximum blade width able to get around that turn.

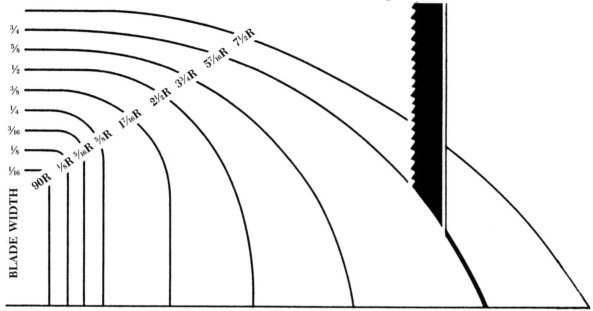

Illus. 2-11. *To determine the width of the blade that should be used, you have to determine the smallest radius of a turn that will be cut. Use this chart to* *determine the widest blade you could use to get around the turn.*

Grain Orientation

Another factor you should consider when choosing a blade is the type of grain the saw blade will encounter during the cut. (See Illus. 2-12.) The best blade to use to crosscut, to cut diagonally, and for multigrain cutting is a standard-tooth blade. (See Illus. 2-13.) A skip-tooth blade also works well on long, gentle curves with the grain, and is often acceptable when making multigrain cuts. (See Illus. 2-14.) A ¼-inch-wide skip-tooth blade with 4 to 6 teeth per inch is usually considered the best all-around blade. A hook-tooth blade is good at long curves cut with the grain, and is especially good at cutting with the grain when you are making straight cuts, such as ripping or resawing. (See Illus. 2-15.)

Illus. 2-12. *The crosscut exposes the end grain of the board. The rip cut exposes the long grain of the board.*

LONG GRAIN

END GRAIN

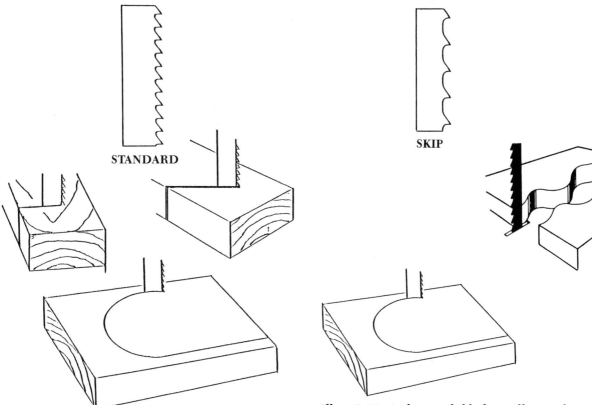

STANDARD

SKIP

Illus. 2-13. *A standard-tooth blade can be used to crosscut and for multi-grain cutting. It gives the smoothest overall cut.*

Illus. 2-14. *A skip-tooth blade is effective for cuts that are either with the grain or against the grain. It does not give as smooth a cut as the standard-tooth blade.*

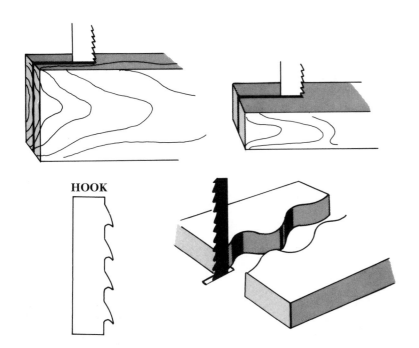

HOOK

Illus. 2-15. *A hook-tooth blade is the best blade to use to cut with the grain. It is also good for straight cuts or gentle curves.*

Folding a Blade

After you have used the blade, you should fold it and store it. There are a number of different techniques for folding the blade. Illus. 2-16 and 2-17 show the two primary techniques. Most people prefer to use the way shown in Illus. 2-16 because they can use both their hands and one foot to hold the blade.

Below are the folding instructions for both techniques.

Technique Number One (Illus. 2-16):
A. Hold one end of the blade with your foot.
B. Hold the other end with your hand and twist it.
C. Use your free hand to hold the blade while you reposition your other hand.
D. Make another twist of the blade in the same direction as the first twist.
E. This creates three loops.
F. Open your hand so that all of the loops are captured.

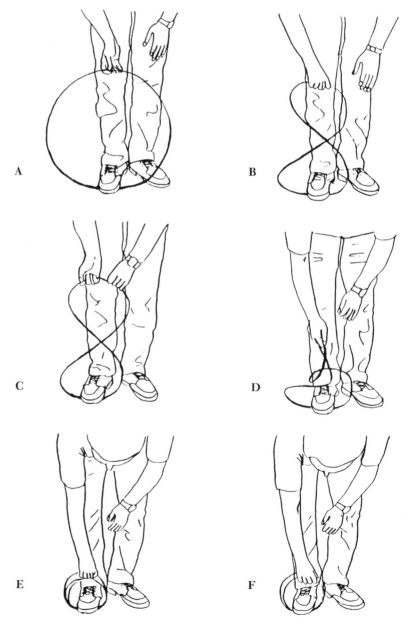

Illus. 2-16. *One technique for folding the blade.*

Technique Number Two (Illus. 2-17):
A. Hold the blade so that your thumbs are pointed in opposite directions.
B. To twist the blade, rotate your hands in opposite directions.
C. Two loops are created.
D. Twist the blade again.
E. The additional twist has created a third loop. The blade is ready for storage.

You can use string or wire to hold the blade in its folded position. Pipe cleaners work very well, and are reusable. (See Illus. 2-18.)

Be careful when unfolding a blade—especially when using wide blades, because they have a lot of spring. Always hold the blade away from you; never try to catch or control it with your body. Hold one loop with one hand, and let the blade recoil at arm's length. Wear gloves. Always turn your face away from an uncoiling blade. Wear eye protection when folding or unfolding blades.

After you unfold the blade, inspect it. Try to avoid using blades with cracks, bends, or kinks.

Illus. 2-17. *A second technique for folding the blade.*

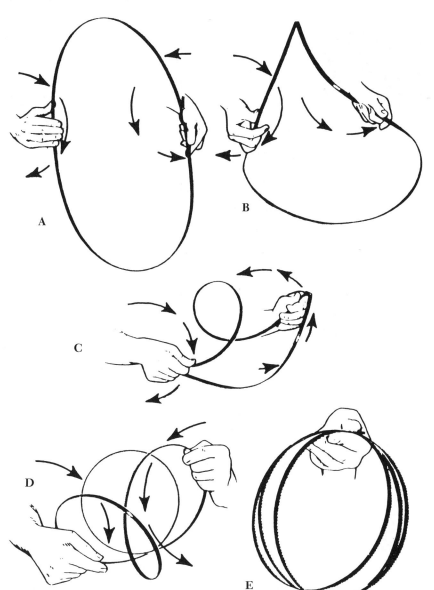

Illus. 2-18. *This blade has been folded and tied to a board with pipe cleaner.*

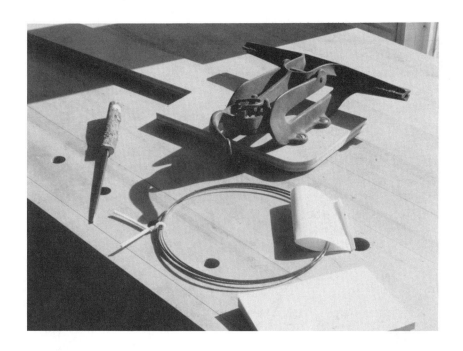

Chapter 3

TUNING AND ADJUSTING YOUR BAND SAW

In order for the band saw to operate at its optimum level, it has to be properly tuned and adjusted. This includes tracking and tensioning the blades, adjusting the thrust-bearing guides and guide posts, and aligning the wheels.

Having a well-tuned and adjusted band saw in your shop has many benefits. It will greatly increase your confidence and your cutting options. It makes the work more efficient and enjoyable. It also makes the wood safer to cut. With a well-tuned band saw, you can rip small pieces that are dangerous to cut on table or radial arm saws. There is no danger that they will kick back with a band saw. If a well-tuned band saw can help prevent an accident, all the attention you give it is certainly worth the effort.

Following is an examination of each of the procedures.

Blade Tracking

Every time you put a new or different blade on the saw, you have to track it. The term "tracking" refers to the act of positioning or balancing the band-saw blade on the wheels. There is no external force that holds the blade on the wheel. It is held on by a combination of two factors. One factor is the outside shape of the wheel. The second factor is the angle of the top wheel. Both are discussed below.

Wheel Shape

The shape of the wheel is determined by the shape of the metal casting on the rim of the wheel. The outside rim of the wheel is covered with a piece of rubber, called a tire, which is between ⅛ and ¼ inch thick. The tire acts as a cushion and a shock absorber. It also protects the blade from contacting the metal wheel, and thus causing damage to the teeth.

Wheels either have a crown or flat shape. (See Illus. 3-1.) The crown exerts a controlling force on the blade which causes it to ride near the middle, but not in the exact middle, of the wheel. A flat wheel is designed so that the operator can track the blade either in the middle of the wheel or towards the front of the wheel. Both systems have advantages and disadvantages.

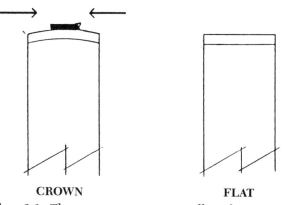

CROWN   **FLAT**

Illus. 3-1. *The crown exerts a controlling force which helps track the blade near the center of the wheel.*

The disadvantage of a crowned wheel is that it provides less surface area between the blade and the tire. This makes it more difficult to track large blades such as a ½-inch blade, which is the best blade to use for straight cuts, especially resawing. Another disadvantage is if the wheels are not perfectly aligned with each other, the crowns on each wheel will compete for control of the blade. This causes vibration and shortens the life of a blade.

A flat wheel provides good support for wide blades, but you have to be more careful tracking the blade. With a flat wheel you can track the blade in various positions on the wheel. Wide blades are best tracked towards the front of the tire. Narrow blades are best tracked towards the middle of the tire.

The main disadvantage of a flat wheel is that when the tire starts to wear, a depression forms in the tire and makes the blades harder to track. You can alleviate this by dressing the tires with sandpaper. This is discussed in the next chapter.

Top-Wheel Angle

The second factor that affects the tracking of a blade is the angle of the top wheel. The angle of the top wheel steers the blade in the direction of the tilt. (See Illus. 3-2.) The usual approach is to tilt the top wheel, usually rearwards, until the blade tracks in the center of the top wheel. (See Illus. 3-3.) This approach is the one that is usually recommended in the owner's manual. It is called "center tracking." (See Illus. 3-4.)

Center tracking works well on blades that are ³⁄₁₆ inch wide or narrower. These blades are flexible, and the misalignment of the wheel doesn't harm the performance or the life expectancy of the blades. However, larger blades—those wider than ¼-inch—are not flexible like the narrower blades. Track these wider blades with the wheels lined up with each other, rather than with the top wheel angled. This is called "coplanar tracking" because the wheels are in a coplanar position (lying in the same plane). (See Illus. 3-5.)

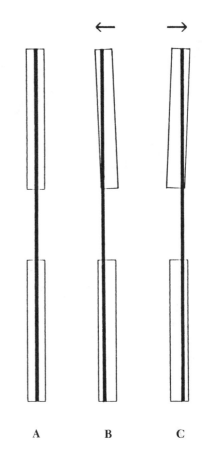

A   B   C

Illus. 3-2. *The angle of the top wheel steers the blade in the direction of the tilt.*

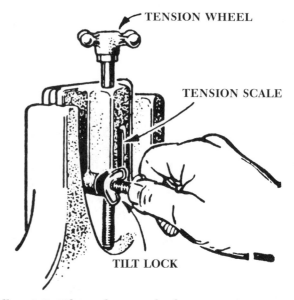

Illus. 3-3. *Tilting the top wheel.*

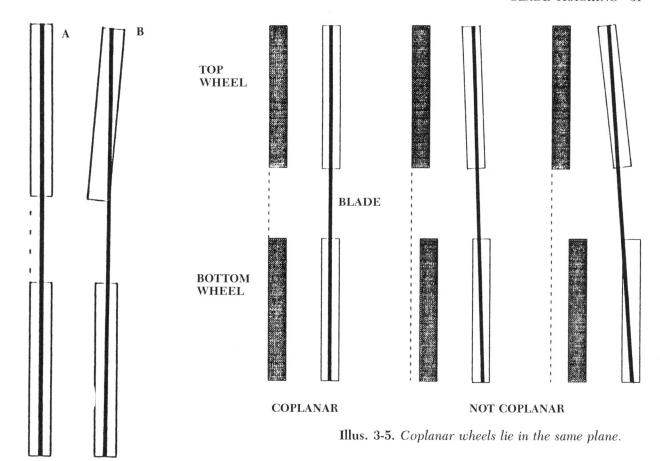

Illus. 3-4. *Use coplanar tracking (B) on blades that are ¼ inch wide or wider. Use center tracking (A) on blades that are ³⁄₁₆ inch wide or narrower.*

Illus. 3-5. *Coplanar wheels lie in the same plane.*

When tracking wide blades, your goal is to allow the blade to run as straight as possible. If the wheels are coplanar, the blade will find its own equilibrium and essentially track itself. With coplanar tracking, the blade exerts the same amount of pressure on the tires at all points of contact. There is no binding, which occurs when you angle the top wheel. The blade will last longer and cut straighter, and will require less tension for good performance.

One of the things that you will notice when you are using coplanar tracking is that the blade will have a tendency to track towards the front of the wheels. The reason why this area is the position of equilibrium is that the front of the blade is narrower than the back of the blade. When the blade is manufactured, the teeth are first ground and then hardened, which causes the front of the

blade to shrink in relationship to the back. The difference between the front and the back is greater on wide blades.

Tracking Procedure

A lot of people do not like to change saw blades, and go to great lengths to avoid doing it. However, to use the band saw to its greatest advantage, you will have to use the appropriate blade and quickly change and track it, a habit that can be easily developed if you are so inclined.

If you use a consistent step-by-step method, tracking should take only a minute or two.

Be careful when using blades, especially wide and sharp ones. Some people prefer to use gloves when handling large blades. Safety glasses are always a good idea. Following are the step-by-step procedures for tracking a blade:

Removing the Blade

1. Unplug the saw.

2. Remove the mechanism for aligning the table halves. It will either be a pin, a bolt, or a front rail.

3. Unscrew the blade guard or open the hinge.

4. Remove the throat plate.

5. Release the tension, thus lowering the top wheel.

6. Expose the wheels by opening or removing the covers.

7. Take the blade off the wheels with both hands, and carefully slide it out of the table slot.

8. Fold the blade.

9. Retract the thrust bearings above and below the table.

10. Loosen the guides on the side of the blade and then retract them, also. This way, you can easily install the next blade without having any obstructions.

Installing the Blade

1. Uncoil the blade. Remember to use gloves and safety glasses. If it is a new blade, it may have oil or dirt on it. The blade may have been oiled to prevent rust. You do not want the oil or dirt touching the workpiece, so remove it before installing the blade. Wipe it off with a rag or a paper towel. Pull the blade through the rag rearwards so that the teeth don't hook.

2. Hold the blade up to the saw. Inspect the teeth. If the teeth are pointed in the wrong direction, you will have to turn the blade inside out. To do this, hold the blade with both hands and rotate it.

3. Hold the blade with both hands, with the teeth edges towards you. Slide it through the table slot and place it on the wheels. Some people like to handle it from the top wheel, because then they are taking advantage of the force of gravity.

4. Position the blade where you want it on the wheels. Then tension it (make it taut between the wheels). Slowly raise the top wheel with the tension knob. Start to rotate the wheels by hand in the normal direction while the blade is still fairly slack. As you do this, watch to determine where the blade wants to track. If the blade is tracking too far forward or backwards, make an adjustment with the tilt mechanism. As you rotate the blade with one hand, increase its tension, or tautness, with the other. (See Illus. 3-6.)

Illus. 3-6. *Simultaneously rotate the blade with one hand and increase its tension with the other. Increase its tension with the tension knob.*

Continue to do this until you have adequate tension. A blade can not be correctly tracked until the tensioning is completed. Never track the blade with the saw running.

5. After the blade has been tracked, replace the cover and the blade guard. Plug in the electrical cord. Turn the saw on for a second, and then turn it off again. Watch to see how the saw runs. If the blade seems to track well, run it under full power. Below are the specific tracking instructions.

Tracking the Blade If you are using *center tracking*, rotate the wheel by hand and angle the top wheel until the blade is tracking in the middle of the top wheel. (See Illus. 3-7.) Make several revolutions of the blade to make sure that the blade stays in the same place on the wheels. Lock the

tilt knob. Center tracking works best on blades that are ³⁄₁₆ inch wide and narrower.

If you are using *coplanar tracking*, align the wheels with a straightedge. (See Illus. 3-8.) Make several revolutions of the blade to make sure that it stays in the same place on the wheels. The blade may or may not track in the center of the top wheel. The blade will usually track towards the front of the wheels. Lock the tilt knob. Tilt the top wheel slightly rearwards if the blade starts to move forward or comes off the front of the saw. Coplanar tracking works best with blades that are ¼ inch wide and wider.

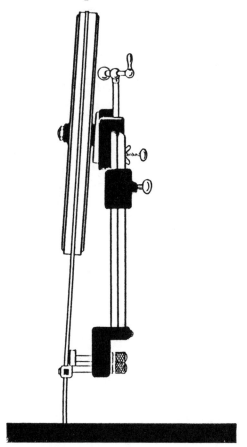

Illus. 3-7. *When center-tracking, rotate the top wheel by hand until the blade tracks in the middle of it.*

Illus. 3-8. *The first step in coplanar tracking is aligning the wheels with a straightedge.*

Adjusting the Band Saw

There are certain parts of the band saw that have to be adjusted so that the band saw can make accurate cuts. Before you learn to adjust them, you should be aware of how they function.

As the workpiece is moved into the blade, a mechanism is needed to prevent the blade from being shoved off the wheels. On most saws, a round wheel bearing called the "thrust bearing"

is used to stop the rearward movement of the blade. (See Illus. 3-9.) There are usually two thrust bearings, one above and one below the table.

"Guides" are paired with each thrust bearing on each side of the blade. The guides prevent the sideways movement, or deflection, of the blade. They also prevent excessive twisting of the blade when it is being used to cut curves.

There are usually four guides, one on each side of the blade above and below the table. (See Illus. 3-9.)

Illus. 3-9. *The thrust bearing is located behind the blade and prevents the blade from being shoved rearwards by the workpiece. The guides are located on each side of the blade, and prevent twisting and deflecting.*

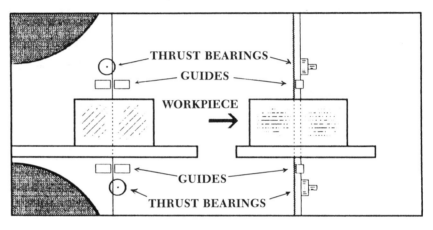

Illus. 3-10. *The guide assembly is a casting that holds the bearings and the guide holder.*

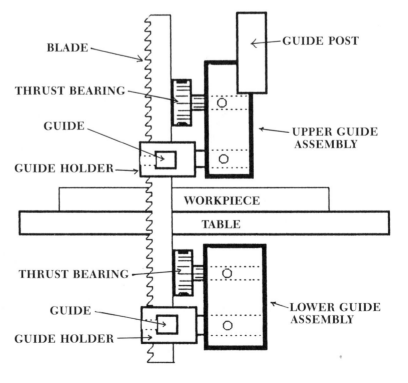

The guides and bearing are held in place by a metal casting called the "guide assembly." There are two guide assemblies: one above and one below the table. (See Illus. 3-10.) The top guide assembly is attached to the guide post, which is movable up and down and is thus adjustable to the thickness of the workpiece.

Each guide assembly has a mechanism for the independent forward-and-rearward movement of the guides and thrust bearing. This guide-assembly design accommodates different blade widths.

The guides are held secure in a unit called the "guide holder." Both guides are held in line with each other so that both move forward and rearward in unison. Each guide is locked in place with a setscrew. (See Illus. 3-11.)

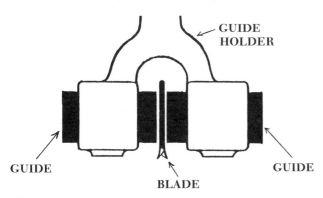

Illus. 3-11. *The guide holder secures the guides and maintains their alignment with each other.*

Adjusting the band saw consists of adjusting the guide post, squaring the table, adjusting the thrust bearings, and adjusting the guide blocks. These procedures take very little time, and are explored below.

Adjusting the Guide Post

The top guide assembly is attached to a movable post that is raised or lowered to accommodate different thicknesses of wood. The post should be adjusted so that there is about ¼ inch of clearance between the bottom of the post and the top of the workpiece. (See Illus. 3-12.) This provides a safety feature and provides maximum support for the blade.

To get a good performance out of the band saw,

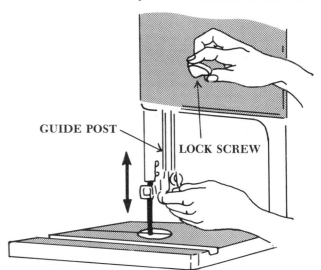

Illus. 3-12. *The guide post is adjustable up and down.*

it is important that the two thrust bearings support the blade equally. This means that the top and bottom thrust bearings must be aligned with each other. Unfortunately, the guide post does not always go straight up and down, thus maintaining the alignment of the bearings. For this reason, it is best to adjust the height of the post *before* adjusting the thrust bearing and the top guide blocks. You should recheck the top thrust bearing and the top guide blocks for alignment each time you raise or lower the post.

Squaring the Table

It is also important that the blade and table be square to each other. Check and readjust the table before adjusting the thrust bearing and the guides. Use a high-quality square for this procedure. (See Illus. 3-13 and 3-14.) Check the squareness frequently.

Most saws have an adjustable mechanism for keeping this table square such as a bolt on the bottom of the table. Adjust the bolt using a trial-and-error method until the blade and table are square.

Adjusting the Thrust Bearings

The next step is to adjust the thrust bearings. Position the blade weld opposite the bearings. The blade is being used as a straightedge, and

Illus. 3-13. *A combination square provides a broad base to check for squareness.*

Illus. 3-14. *The table is adjustable with a bolt or screw. The Sears band saw is adjustable through the top. If you are using a small square, use the broadest surface on the table.*

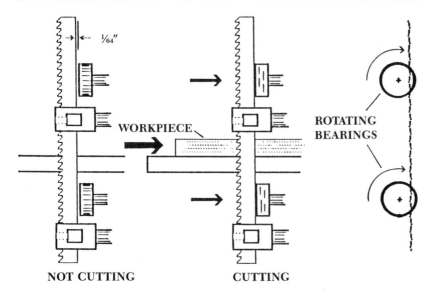

Illus. 3-15. *The blade should not touch the thrust bearings unless the saw is cutting.*

the weld is the least straight part of the blade.

Position the two thrust bearings about 1/64 inch (.015″) behind the blade. (See Illus. 3-15.) When the cut begins, the blade moves rearwards and contacts the thrust bearings. When the cutting stops, the blade should move forward again, and the bearings should stop rotating. You can use a feeler gauge or a dollar bill folded twice to determine the correct space between the blade and the bearings.

Adjusting the Guide Blocks

Next, adjust the guide blocks. As mentioned, the four guide blocks are held in place by the guide holders that are paired with each thrust bearing above and below the table. (See Illus. 3-9.) Some manufacturers use bearings instead of solid metal guides. In recent years, a nonmetal replacement guide block called Cool Blocks has become very popular. Cool Blocks are a patented fibre with a dry lubricant that greatly decreases the friction between the blade and the blocks. This decreases the heat generated by the blade and thus increases the life of the blade.

Another advantage is that the Cool Blocks can be placed in contact with the blade. This decreases twist and deflection, and improves the accuracy of the band-saw cut.

Place the metal guide blocks about .004 inch away from the blade. This is the thickness of a piece of paper, so you can use a dollar bill as a spacer. (See Illus. 3-16.) You must be careful when doing this. The distance between the gullet and the front of the guide block should be about 1/64 inch because the blade will flex backwards during the cut. (See Illus. 3-17.)

Rounding the Blade Back One step that improves blade performance and blade life is to round the back of the blade with a stone. (A stone is used to grind, shape, or smooth a tool.) A

Illus. 3-17 (right). *When the saw has stopped cutting, the blade will spring back to its original position. When adjusting the guides, make sure that the distance between the back of the gullet and the guide is the same as the distance between the blade and the thrust bearing.*

Illus. 3-16. *Paper money is about .004 inch thick and is a good measuring instrument.*

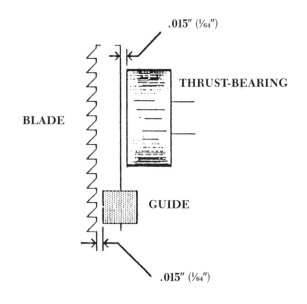

.015″ (1/64″)

THRUST-BEARING

BLADE

GUIDE

.015″ (1/64″)

round blade back creates smooth interaction between the bearing and the blade. If the blade rotates slightly, there is no sharp blade corner to dig into the thrust bearing. Also, the rounding process smooths the weld. A blade with a round back makes tight turns better because the round back has smooth interaction with the saw kerf. (See Illus. 3-18.)

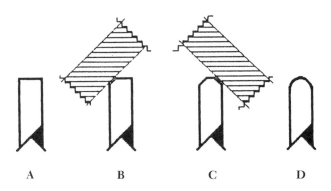

A   B   C   D

Illus. 3-19. *To round the back of a blade, first file the corner, as shown in B and C. Then slowly rotate the file around the back, as shown in D. This process takes about two or three minutes.*

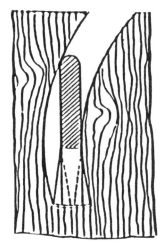

Illus. 3-18. *The round blade interacts smoothly with the edge of the saw kerf (cut).*

After the guides have been adjusted, hold the stone against the corner of the blade for about a minute. (See Illus. 3-19.) *Wear safety glasses when rounding the blade.* Then do the same thing on the opposite corner.

Next, slowly move the stone to round the back. The more pressure you put on the back, the faster you will remove the metal. Be careful that the inside of the machine is free from sawdust, because sparks could start a fire.

On small blades such as a ⅛- or 1/16-inch blade, the pressure on the back of the blade may bring the blade forward off the front of the wheels. To prevent this, it is best to feed wood into the blade during the rounding process. Pass the wood underneath the elevated stone. This keeps the blade in contact with the thrust bearing. (See Illus. 3-20.)

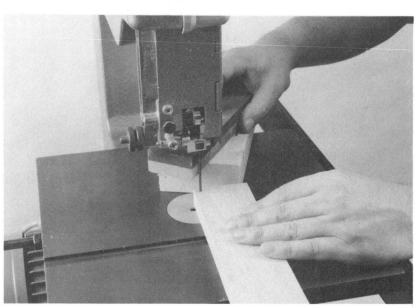

Illus. 3-20. *Feed the wood into a ⅛- or 1/16-inch-wide blade while rounding it.*

Using Narrow Blades Until recently, the narrowest blade that was available for the band saw was ⅛ inch wide. The latest development for band saws is a blade that is only ¹⁄₁₆ inch wide. This blade makes extremely tight turns, similar to those made by an expensive scroll-saw blade. (See Illus. 3-21.)

A band saw that can make very tight turns has an advantage in that it can cut much faster, especially in thick, hard stock. That is why the ¹⁄₁₆-inch blade is becoming very popular, even with those who already have a scroll saw.

To use the smaller blades successfully, you will have to make some changes in the standard adjustment procedure. It is necessary to replace the metal guides. Cool Blocks seem to work best.

Place these blocks just behind the gullets. (See Illus. 3-22.)

As mentioned in the previous section, you should round the back of a small band-saw blade. Also, use center tracking to track the blade. Keep the top guide assembly about an inch above the work. This will allow the blade to flex rearwards slightly during the cut. This eliminates the possibility that the blade will be forced to make a sharp angle under the top thrust bearing. The thrust bearing should rest against the back of the blade with no space between the bearing and the blade (See Illus. 3-23). This gives the small blades added support.

A ⅛- and ¹⁄₁₆-inch blade last significantly longer when the guide is raised. However, this exposes

Illus. 3-21. *A ¹⁄₁₆-inch blade cuts much faster than a scroll saw blade, particularly in thick hard wood such as the two-inch hard maple shown here.*

Illus. 3-22. *This band saw is fitted with a ¹⁄₁₆-inch blade and Cool Blocks. Cool Blocks are replacement guide blocks that allow the use of small blades and prolong normal blade life.*

Illus. 3-23. *Position the thrust bearings ¹⁄₆₄ inch behind the blade.*

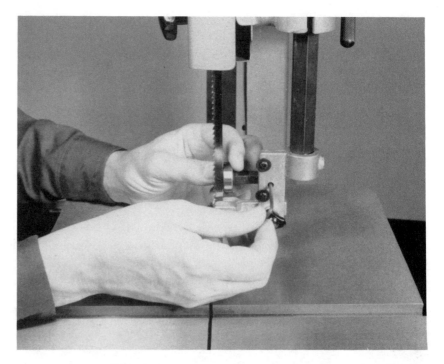

Illus. 3-24. *You can extend the life of narrow blades if you follow a few simple rules. When using a narrow blade such as a ⅛- or ¹⁄₁₆-inch blade, keep the top guide about an inch above the work-piece. This will allow the blade to flex rearwards slightly during the cut. Cool Blocks should be used because with these blade guides there is less destructive blade heat generated. This is especially important with small blades because there is less metal to act as a heat conductor. The cooler the blade, the longer it will last.*

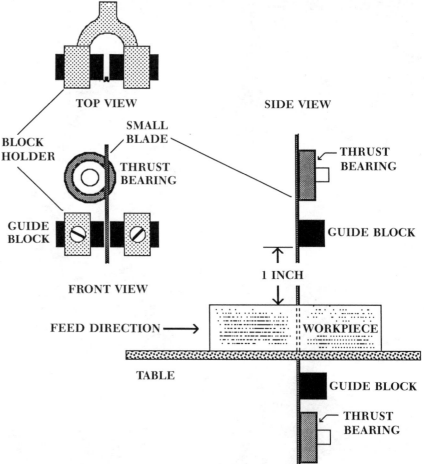

about an inch of blade, which could be a potential hazard, *so use extra caution.* (See Illus. 3-24.)

Aligning Band-Saw Wheels

Aligning band-saw wheels is a very simple procedure that should take only a couple of minutes to accomplish. They may or may not be already aligned. The first thing to do is to check. Use the following steps to check, and then to align the band-saw wheels:

1. *Tension the blade.* Tension the widest blade that you can use on your saw. Tensioning is stretching the blade taut between the wheels. The ½-inch blade is the largest practical size to use on a consumer band saw. Use the tension scale on your band saw. (See Illus. 3-25.)

2. *Make sure that the wheels are parallel to*

Illus. 3-25. *Tension the widest blade that you will use. Here a ½-inch-wide blade is being tensioned on a Sears band saw.*

each other. With a straightedge, check to determine if the wheels are parallel with each other. You may have to angle the top wheel to get them parallel.

Put the straightedge in the middle of the wheels. If it touches the top and bottom of both wheels, then the wheels are parallel and in line—they are coplanar. (See Illus. 3-26.) If this is the case, you do not have to align them.

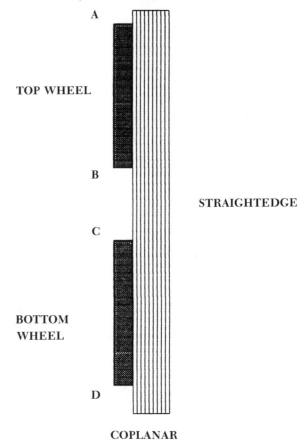

Illus. 3-26. *The wheels are coplanar if the straightedge touches the tops and bottoms of both wheels. These positions are designated in the drawings as A,B,C, and D.*

If the wheels are not in alignment, the straightedge will not touch the top and bottom of both wheel points. (See Illus. 3-27.) Instead, it will either touch the top and bottom of the top wheel or the top and bottom of the lower wheel. In either case, you will have to move one of the wheels to make both wheels coplanar.

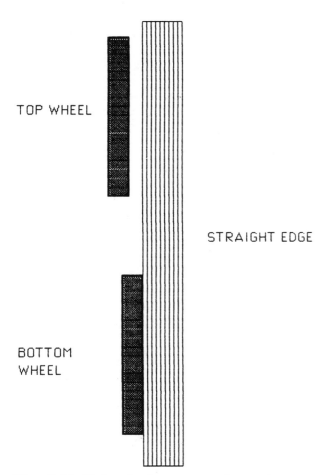

Illus. 3-27. *If the wheels are not coplanar, the straightedge will only touch one wheel.*

3. *Measure the misalignment.* It is important to know how far one of the wheels has to be moved to achieve coplanar alignment. This is essential if you are going to achieve coplanar alignment by adding or removing washers from behind the wheel.

Measure the misalignment at the top and bottom of the wheel that is not touching the straightedge. (See Illus. 3-28–3-30.) The measurements at both points should be the same. If they are not exactly the same, angle the top wheel until they are. (See Illus. 3-31 and 3-32.) Once they are the same, that amount (X) is the distance the wheel needs to move to align the wheels. In the situation shown in Illus. 3-28–3-30, move the top wheel forward X amount to achieve alignment.

4. *Make the adjustment.* On Sears and Inca models, the adjustment is made with a movable bottom wheel. (See Illus. 3-33.) This is the easiest and most convenient way. The bottom wheel is mounted on a shaft in a key way (a groove on the shaft that prevents the wheel from spinning on the shaft), and the wheel is locked in place with a setscrew. When making the adjustment, loosen the screw and move the wheel to the desired amount.

On the Delta and Taiwanese band saws, the adjustment is made on the top wheel, which is mounted on a threaded shaft and held secure with a nut. (See Illus. 3-34.) To make the adjust-

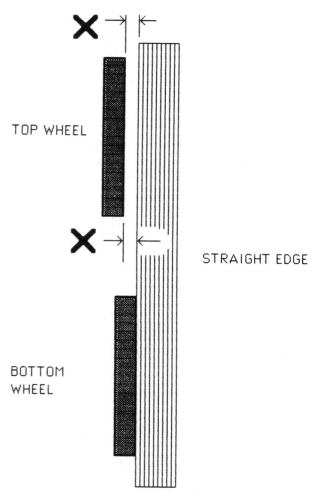

Illus. 3-28. *It is important to know how much to move the wheel to make the wheels coplanar. Measure this amount from the top and bottom of the wheel.*

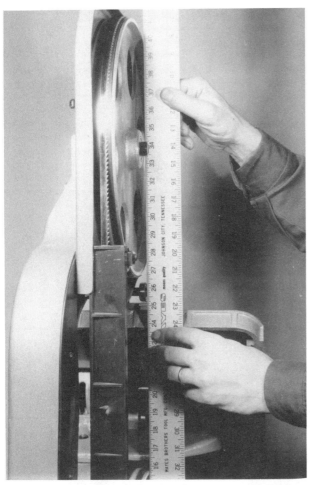

Illus. 3-29. *Hold the straightedge against the bottom wheel.*

Illus. 3-30. *With a straightedge against the bottom wheel, use a ruler to measure the distance between the top wheel and the straightedge. You may have to hold the straightedge against the bottom wheel with your knee.*

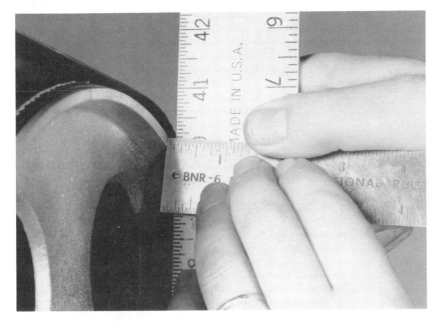

Illus. 3-31. *With a fine ruler, make the final measurement.*

Illus. 3-32. *The bottom measurement should be exactly the same as the top. If it isn't, the top wheel should be tilted until it is the same on the top and the bottom.*

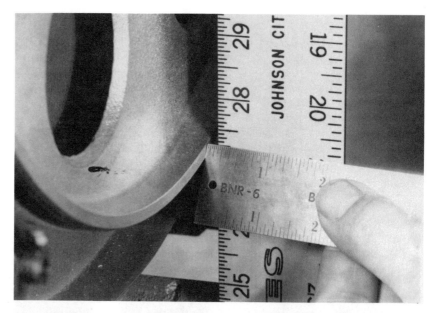

Illus. 3-33. *You can adjust a Sears band saw by moving the bottom wheel. A screw holds the wheel on the shaft.*

Illus. 3-34. *You can adjust a Delta and a Taiwanese band saw by moving the top wheel, which is held in place with a nut. First, remove the nut, and then the wheel. Add or subtract the washer behind the wheel to make the adjustment.*

ment, unscrew the nut and then remove the wheels; this will expose the washers. Make the alignment by either adding or removing washers. You can buy additional washers at hardware dealers.

After the first alignment, always rotate the wheels several times to make sure that the blade is tracking; then recheck the alignment.

Don't be afraid to realign the wheels often. Think of the procedure as just another adjustment that should be made. After you have aligned the wheels a couple of times, it will become very simple to do. And you'll notice how useful it is—the minute that it takes for alignment is a small price to pay for good performance.

Chapter 4

MAINTENANCE AND SAFETY PROCEDURES

Maintenance Procedures

There are three main areas that require maintenance: the wheel tires, the thrust bearings, and the guide blocks. The tires are made of rubber, and wear just as a car tire does. They wear in the middle, which causes a concavity in the tire. This is especially true of tires that are flat. The concavity makes it hard to track the blade.

For this reason, it is important to maintain the original shape of the tires. This can be done by sanding the wheel with 100-grit sandpaper. To do this, first remove the blade. Never sand the tires with the blade on the machine. Sand the bottom tire with the saw running. (See Illus. 4-1.)

To rotate the top wheel, use a drill with a sanding drum that is about 1½ inches in diameter. (See Illus. 4-2.) You may feel more comfortable sanding the bottom tire if you use sandpaper attached to a stick. (See Illus. 4-3.)

Illus. 4-1. *The wheel tire should be cleaned and the original shape restored occasionally. Here, medium-grit sandpaper is being used to clean and shape the bottom tire while the saw is running.*

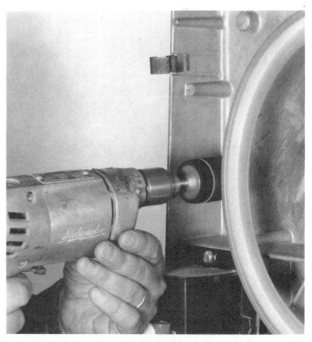

Illus. 4-2. *The top wheel does not have a source of power, so an outside source such as a drill can be used to rotate the wheel. Here a drill with a 1¼-inch-diameter sanding drum is being used to rotate the wheel.*

Illus. 4-3. *You may feel more comfortable sanding the band-saw wheel if the sandpaper is mounted on a stick.*

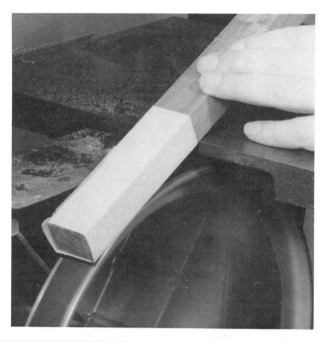

Illus. 4-4. *The bearing on the left is new. The bearing in the middle has a scar on top of it. The bearing on the right is completely destroyed.*

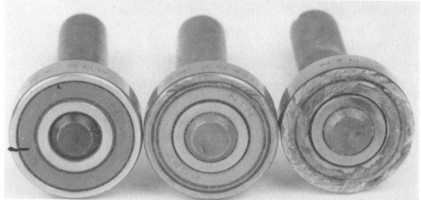

Illus. 4-5. *Some bearings are attached to the saw with a screw.*

Illus. 4-6. *Reversing the bearing exposes a new surface.*

Thrust bearings can wear or become scarred. (See Illus. 4-4.) Some of these bearings can be removed from the shaft and reversed, thus providing a new surface. (See Illus. 4-5 and 4-6.)

Check the rotation of the bearings frequently. If the bearings do not rotate easily, they should be replaced. Order the new bearings from your dealer or the manufacturer.

Guide blocks can also wear and can become rounded. Cool Blocks wear slightly faster than the metal guides. Both types of blocks should be resurfaced as needed. Resurface the blocks with a file or a power disc or a belt sander.

Diagnosing Problems

There are a number of problems that band-saw users experience. These problems include blade breakage, crooked cuts, and vibration. There are a number of reasons for the various problems. The following is a list of the problems, the reasons for them, and solutions:

Blade Breakage

Reason	*Solution*
A. Excessively high feed rate.	Slow the feed rate.
B. Guides or bearings are poorly adjusted.	Readjust the guides and bearings. (See Chapter 3.)
C. Blade tension is too high.	Decrease the blade tension. Use only as much tension as you need to perform an operation.
D. Band is too thick in relationship to the diameter of the wheels and the sawing speed.	Use a narrower band.
E. Poor weld.	Replace blade.

Crooked Sawing

Reason	*Solution*
A. Guides and bearings are poorly adjusted.	Readjust bearings and guides properly. (See Chapter 3.)
B. Blade tension is too low.	Increase the blade tension to the recommended amount.
C. Dull blade.	Have blade sharpened or replace blade.
D. Pitch is too fine.	Use blade with coarser pitch (less teeth per inch).
E. Damaged teeth.	Replace blade.
F. Fence poorly aligned.	Realign fence.

Safety Procedures

The band saw is a popular tool because it is easy to use and because it is so versatile. It is also fairly safe to use. However, you should not take this for granted. *Read the following safety rules carefully, and observe each and every one.*

1. Read and understand the instruction manual that comes with the saw before operating it.

2. If you are still not thoroughly familiar with the operation of the band saw, get advice from a qualified person.

3. Make sure that the machine is properly grounded, and that the wiring codes are followed.

4. Do not operate the band saw while under the influence of drugs, alcohol, medication, or if tired.

5. Always wear eye protection (safety glasses or a face shield) and hearing protection. (See Illus. 4-7 and 4-8.)

6. Wear a dust mask. (See Illus. 4-9.) Long-term exposure to the fine dust created by the band saw is not healthy.

7. Remove your tie, rings, watch, and all jewelry. Roll up your sleeves. You do not want anything to get caught in the saw.

8. Make sure that the guards are in place, and use them at all times. The guards protect you from coming into contact with the blade.

9. Make sure that the saw-blade teeth point downwards towards the table.

10. Adjust the upper blade guard so that it is about ¼ inch above the material being cut.

11. Make sure that the blade has been properly tensioned and tracked.

12. Stop the machine before removing the scrap pieces from the table.

13. Always keep your hands and fingers away from the blade.

14. Make sure that you use the proper size and type of blade.

15. Hold the workpiece firmly against the table. Do not attempt to saw stock that does not have a flat surface, unless a suitable support is used.

16. Use a push stick at the end of a cut. (See Illus. 4-10.) This is the most dangerous time, because the cut is complete and the blade is exposed. Push sticks are commercially available.

17. Hold the wood firmly, and feed it into the blade at a moderate speed. (See Illus. 4-11.)

18. Turn off the machine if you have to back the material out of an uncompleted or jammed cut.

Illus. 4-7. *Protect your eyes with either safety glasses or goggles. Most woodworkers prefer safety glasses.*

Illus. 4-8. *Although the band saw is quieter than most woodworking machines, wear hearing protection. Noise creates hearing loss and makes you more tired. The ear inserts shown on the left are becoming increasingly more popular. The hearing muffs shown on the right work well but are bulky, especially when used with glasses.*

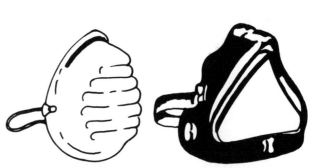

Illus. 4-9. *Because the band saw creates fine dust, you should wear a dust mask. The model shown on the left is disposable. The one shown on the right is plastic and features a replaceable filter.*

Illus. 4-10. *Keep a push stick on the table. This way, if you need it, it is quickly within reach. At the end of the cut, use it to push the workpiece forward.*

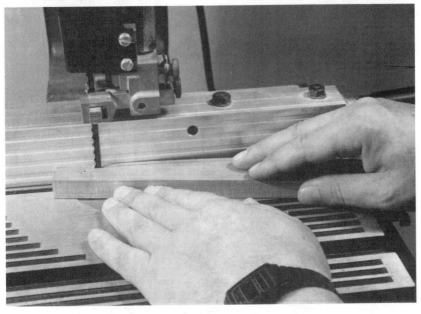

Illus. 4-11. *Make sure that you feed the wood into the blade at a moderate speed. You can use two hands to pull the workpiece through the cut.*

Chapter 5

BASIC SAWING GUIDELINES AND CUTTING TECHNIQUES

Sawing Guidelines

There are several general sawing guidelines that should always be followed when you use a band saw. They are:

1. Feed the work gently into the blade. Do not force the work or bend or twist the blade. Remember that you must be feeding the wood forward when you are making a turn, especially a tight turn. A gentle, smooth rhythm will give the best results.

2. When sawing, you usually follow a line on the work. A pencil line works best because it does not leave a permanent stain, and it can be erased. Saw near the outside of the line, but not on it. (See Illus. 5-1.) This way, the line will still be intact if you decide to sand or plane the edge, and you can still see the desired shape.

3. Use both hands to feed the wood into the blade. (See Illus. 5-2.) Keep them on opposite sides of the workpiece. Never cross your hands. If you are in an awkward position, keep one hand

Illus. 5-1. *Saw near, but not on the pencil line. Sand to the line to get the final edge.*

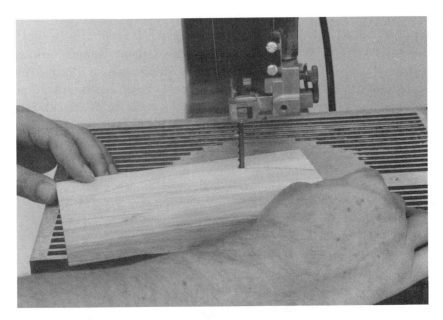

Illus. 5-2. *Use both hands to feed the work into the blade. Keep your hands on opposite sides of the workpiece.*

on the work and move the other hand. Always keep your fingers away from the pencil line, especially at the end of the cut.

4. Use a jig or a clamp to hold odd-shaped or small pieces during the sawing process. (See Illus. 5-3.). Small pieces are more dangerous to cut than large pieces because your fingers are closer to the blade.

5. Think ahead and plan your saw cuts. Al-though the band saw is easy to use, it does require proper technique to use the saw efficiently. There are some situations that it is best to avoid, such as having to back out of long, curved cuts. This can cause the blade to move forward off the saw wheels. If you must back out, turn the saw off first. You can also tilt the top wheel backwards slightly. This will decrease the likelihood of the saw blade coming forward off the wheels when you back out.

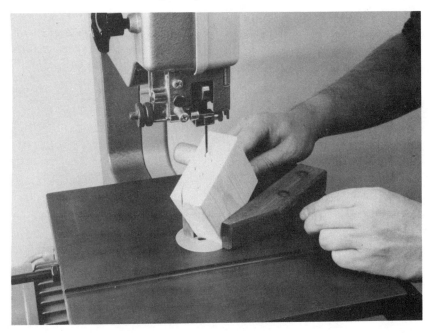

Illus. 5-3. *Use a hand-screw clamp to hold the workpiece when the piece doesn't rest flat on the table.*

Cutting Techniques

The following advice will prove useful in many cutting conditions. It will help you to make certain cuts more efficiently and avoid certain situations that many band-saw users find themselves trapped in.

Release Cuts

Not only is it possible to paint yourself into a corner, you can also band-saw yourself into a corner. A release cut is used to prevent such a situation from occurring. It is made to meet with the end of a long cut. It is used so that the waste piece can be easily separated from the workpiece. (See Illus. 5-4–5-10.)

Illus. 5-4. *The release cut meets with the end of a long cut. Because the workpiece was accurately squared, the release cut and the edge off the board are parallel.*

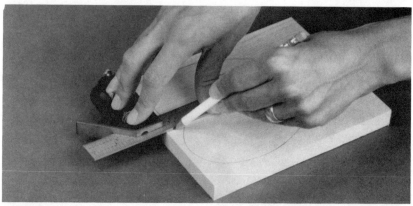

Illus. 5-5. *Release cuts should be as straight as possible. A straight cut makes it easier to retract the workpiece. Mark the cut path with a ruler or square.*

Illus. 5-6. *Make the release cut first. The second cut, as shown here, should end at the release cut.*

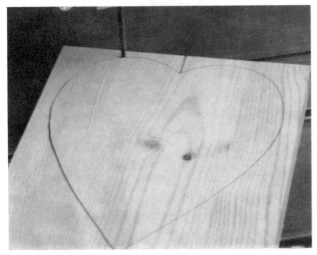

Illus. 5-7. *Make the cut by following the line.*

Illus. 5-8. *The cut intersects with the release cut, which frees the waste piece.*

Illus. 5-9. *Cut the opposite side in a similar fashion.*

Illus. 5-10. *The completed cut.*

Turning Holes

Turning holes, like release cuts, make it easier to remove waste wood. (See Illus. 5-11–5-17.) Turning holes are drilled at key positions in the workpiece. The turning hole can serve as a smooth curve in a pattern such as the one shown in Illus. 5-12. The holes and the straight cuts are made first. The rest of the material is the waste material.

Turning holes are also used at key locations to give the operator more space to rotate the workpiece around the saw blade. (See Illus. 5-13 and 5-15.) They help you to cut out complex patterns more quickly.

Illus. 5-11. *Turning holes can be used to improve the efficiency and accuracy of the band-saw cut. A good example is the letter F.*

Illus. 5-12. *Make the straight cuts with a rip fence.*

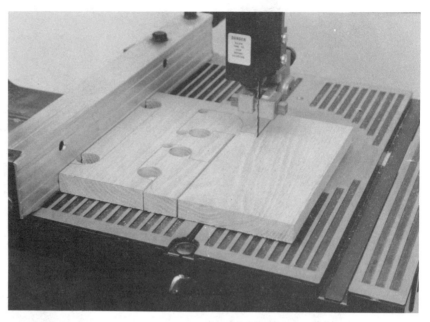

Illus. 5-13. *The hole is big enough so that the workpiece can be rotated freely around the blade.*

Illus. 5-14. *Remove the large waste pieces first.*

Illus. 5-15. *You can trim the small pieces later.*

Illus. 5-16. *Remove the small pieces last.*

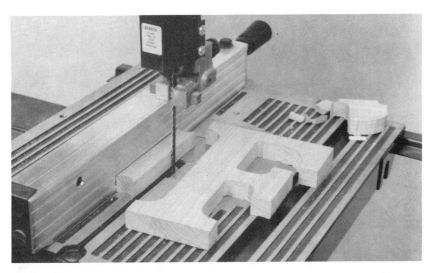

Illus. 5-17. *This completed letter is ready for sanding. The turning holes improve the quality of this job.*

Cutting a Square Inside Corner

Unless you are using a narrow blade, it is difficult to make a square inside corner. In this situation, it is best to make as many straight cuts as possible into the corners. Then back up and make a turn. Last, cut the waste out of the corners. (See Illus. 5-18.)

Circular Cuts

When making a sharp curve, it is often useful to cut past the corner and make a circular cut in the waste area. (See Illus. 5-19.) Continue the cut into the corner. This cut will function like a release cut. Then back up the workpiece and make another cut along the opposite side. This cut will release the waste. (See Illus. 5-20.)

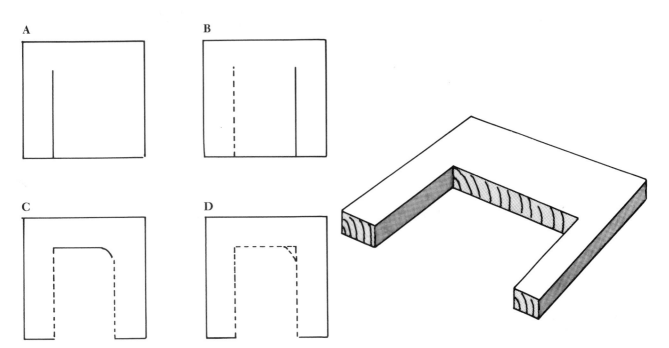

Illus. 5-18. *The four diagrams above show how to remove waste from this shape. Make the straight cuts first, as shown in A and B. B is a release cut* for the curved cut, C. D is a straight cut which removes the waste from the corner.

Illus. 5-19. *When making a sharp curve, it is often useful to make a circular cut.*

Illus. 5-20. *Continue the cut into the corner. It will release a half-circle of waste, which will fall through the throat plate into the band saw. It is important that the waste piece falls opposite the bottom wheel. If the waste piece falls between the blade and the wheel, it can kink or break the wheel.*

Nibbling

Nibbling is using the band-saw blade to remove small pieces of material. It is a procedure often used on tight curves. Small pieces of the material are cut away. This creates room for the blade, so that you can rotate the workpiece without having to twist the blade body. (See Illus. 5-21–5-28.)

Tight Turns with Wide Blades

There will be times when you will have to make a tight turn, but do not want to change to a narrower blade. You can make tight outside curves with a series of straight cuts. Inside curves can be made with a series of release cuts. (See Illus. 5-29.)

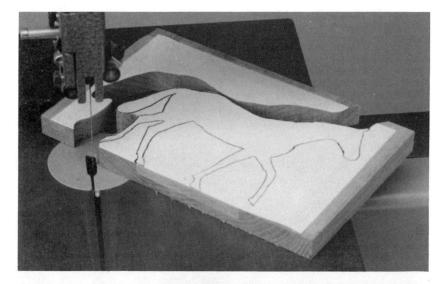

Illus. 5-21. *Nibbling is the technique of backing the workpiece up and making multiple cuts that are the width of the blade. This creates enough room so that the workpiece can be rotated without your having to twist the blade. This technique is useful in situations such as cutting patterns.*

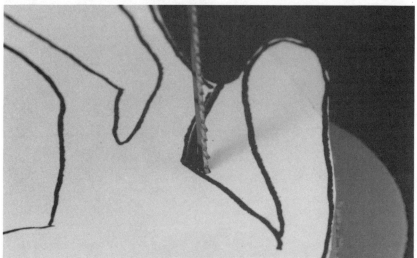

Illus. 5-22. *The corner is too square to allow the blade to rotate, so the first step is to make a straight cut into the corner. Then back the workpiece up and make multiple cuts the width of the blade, as shown here.*

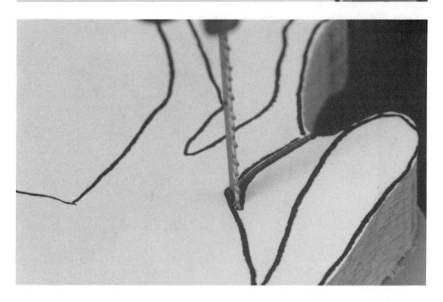

Illus. 5-23. *Then rotate the workpiece so that the blade is in line with the pencil line.*

Illus. 5-24. *Next, make a straight cut into the corner. Place tape over the previous cut to keep the pattern in place.*

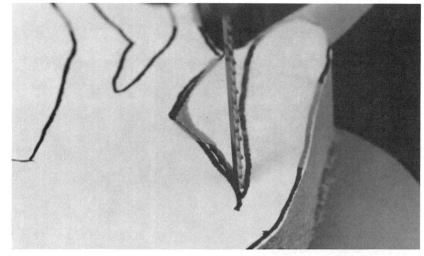

Illus. 5-25. *"Nibble" the corner out with the band-saw blade.*

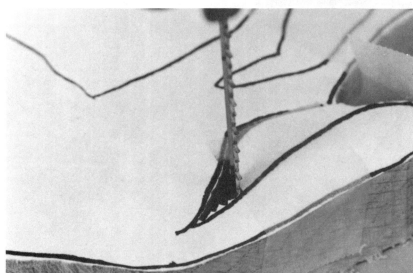

Illus. 5-26. *Nibbling creates a rough surface. Cut along the pencil line with the blade to remove the rough surface.*

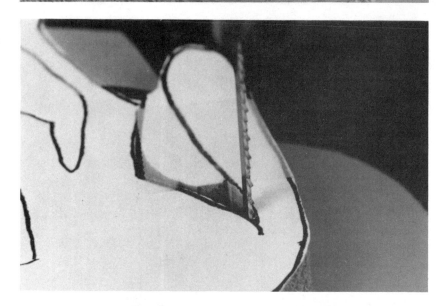

Illus. 5-27. *Next, rotate the workpiece into the space that has been created.*

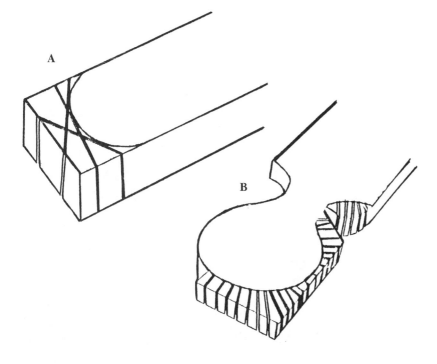

Illus. 5-28. *Finish the cut and remove the waste piece.*

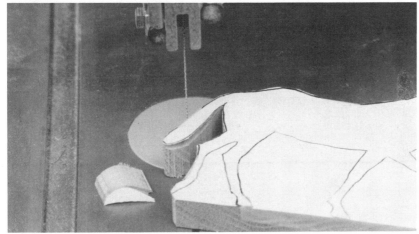

Illus. 5-29. *A. Inside curves can be made with a series of release cuts. B. Outside curves can be made with a series of straight cuts.*

Chapter 6

USING PATTERNS AND TEMPLATES

Patterns

A pattern is the shape of the desired item that you plan on making. It can be drawn directly on the workpiece, or it can be drawn or copied on a piece of paper which is then attached to the workpiece. (See Illus. 6-1.) The paper can be taped in place, or it can be attached with an adhesive such as rubber cement. (See Illus. 6-2.)

Types of Pattern

Full Pattern The full pattern is used when the shape óf the object is not symmetrical (that is, its proportions are not balanced). It is important to consider the direction of the wood's grain when laying out a pattern on the piece of wood. Illus. 6-3 shows the full pattern of a horse. The wood's

Illus. 6-1. *A maple leaf was the pattern for this band-sawn box.*

Illus. 6-2. *Rubber cement holds the pattern firmly to the workpiece. Put the cement only on the pattern, not on the workpiece. After cutting the pattern, peel the paper off.*

Illus. 6-3. *The grain of the wood runs along the length of this pattern.*

grain runs the length of the pattern. The two weakest areas are the tops of the two middle legs because the pattern runs across the grain rather than with the grain. These areas are the places that are most likely to break. In a situation where there are a lot of weak areas, consider using plywood. Plywood is very strong when used in narrow sections.

Half-Pattern When the object is symmetrical, a half-pattern is the best pattern to use. A half-pattern is only half of the shape. You can use the same pattern for both sides of the object by drawing one side and then flipping the pattern over. A simple example would be the pattern of the tree shown in Illus. 6-4. Illus. 6-5 shows a letter holder, a pencil holder, and a knockdown book shelf that were made with a half-pattern.

Quarter-Pattern When the object has four corners that are the same, such as a ellipse, a quarter-pattern is useful. (See Illus. 6-6.) The pattern is flipped left to right, and then top to bottom.

Double Pattern When the object has the same profile from two adjacent sides, the pattern can be used twice. An example of this is the pattern of a cabriole leg shown in Illus. 6-7.

Compound Sawing When there is a pattern on adjacent sides, two series or cuts are needed to release the workpiece. The cabriole leg shown in Illus. 6-7 and the boat shown in Illus. 6-8 were compound-sawed. After sawing the pattern on one side, reattach the waste pieces which contain the pattern for the adjacent side to the workpiece so that the pattern can be cut again. Use nails, hot-melt glue, or tape to reattach the separated piece. Make sure that you plan ahead. Planning ahead makes it easier for you to make the cuts. For example, it is easier to make the last series of cuts on the boat when it is lying flat rather than on its side.

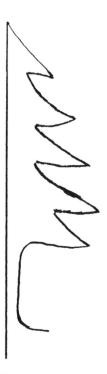

Illus. 6-4. *This half-pattern represents half of a tree.*

Illus. 6-5. *The letter holder, pencil holder, and knockdown book shelf shown here were made with a half-pattern.*

Illus. 6-6. *This ellipse was drawn with a French curve in a manner similar to that used to make quarter-patterns.*

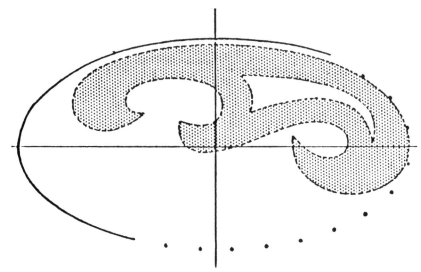

Illus. 6-7. *The same pattern is used on two adjacent sides of this cabriole leg.*

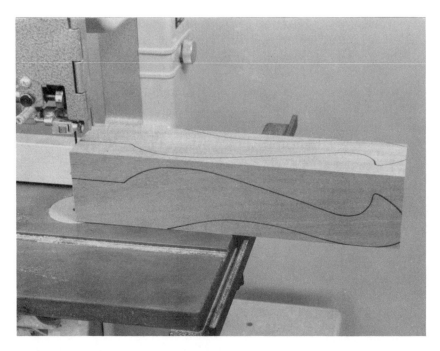

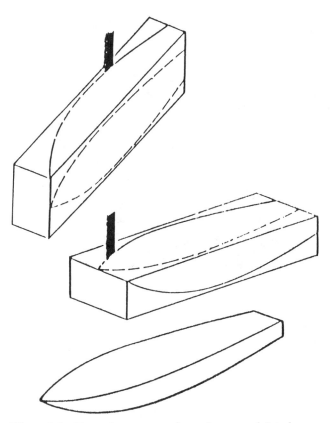

Illus. 6-8. *Here the pattern for a boat-model is being compound-sawed. Compound sawing is when a pattern is cut from two adjacent sides. The second cut or series of cuts is made with the piece resting on its widest surface.*

Creating Patterns There are a number of ways to make patterns. If you are repairing or replacing a part from a piece of furniture, you can trace the part onto a piece of paper or you can glue broken pieces back together to form a pattern. You can also use a profile gauge or curved rulers to transfer shapes. (See Illus. 6-9 and 6-10.)

Changing the Size of Patterns

There are times when you want to change the size of a pattern. The easiest way to do this is to use a photocopier to either enlarge or reduce the pattern. (See Illus. 6-11.) New photocopiers can expand or shrink patterns in one-percent amounts.

A pantograph is a mechanical device that is used to change the scale of a drawing. (See Illus. 6-12.) It is very easy to use. Draw the enlargement or reduction directly onto the workpiece or onto paper. The follower point, shown as A in Illus. 6-12, is guided along the original design, while the pencil point, shown as B, automatically recreates the outline in the exact size and desired proportions.

Because of space limitations, patterns that are offered in magazines and books are often printed in a reduced size. Generally, the pattern is drawn

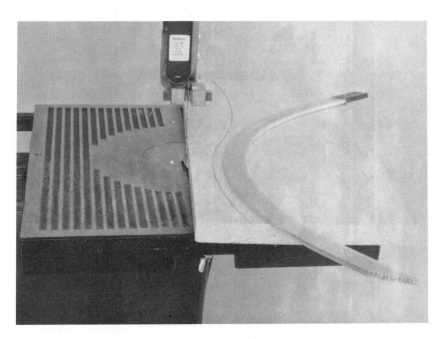

Illus. 6-9. *A curved ruler is useful for laying out a pattern.*

Illus. 6-10. *A profile gauge can be used to transfer a pattern with a curve.*

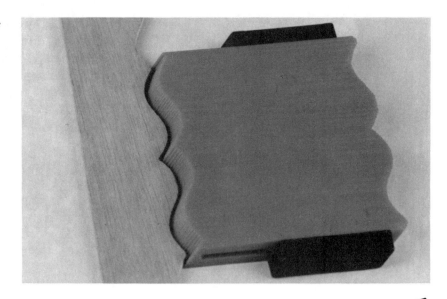

Illus. 6-11. *A photocopier was used to change the size of this design. The three sizes on the left are 93, 74, and 65 percent of the original. The two large designs on the right are 115 and 124 percent of the original, which is on the bottom right.*

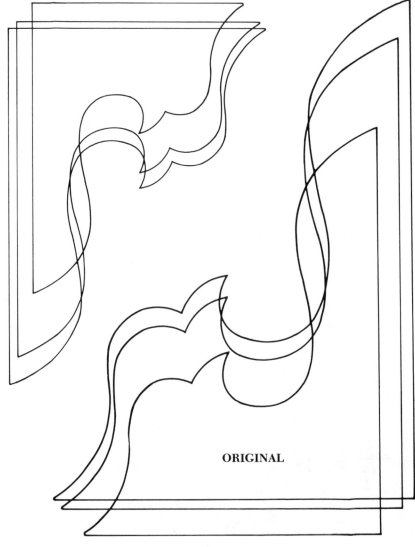

ORIGINAL

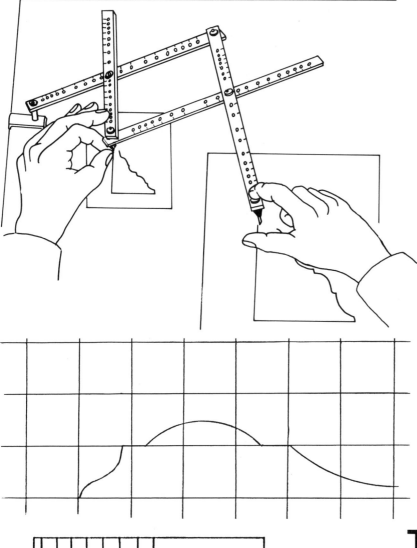

Illus. 6-12. *A pantograph is a mechanical device used to either enlarge or reduce a drawing. (Drawing courtesy of Lee Valley Tools, L.T.D., Ottawa, Canada)*

Illus. 6-13. *Because of space limitations in books and magazines, patterns are often printed in a reduced size with a grid. To make the pattern, make a large grid or use graph paper which already has a grid. Using the intersecting lines as a reference, transfer the pattern to the larger grid.*

Templates

on a grid, which helps to break the pattern down into small, easily transferred components. To enlarge the pattern, you can either make a grid on a piece of paper or use a sheet of graph paper (which already has grids). Using the intersecting lines as a reference, transfer the pattern using corresponding dots. (See Illus. 6-13.) It may be helpful to number the lines in both directions on both the large and the small pattern. Use a French curve to connect the dots forming the lines of the desired pattern.

Paper patterns are not very durable. If you are going to use a pattern often, it is worthwhile to make a template out of a durable material such as Masonite™ (a type of fibreboard), plywood, or plastic. Then use the template to trace the pattern directly onto the workpiece. (See Illus. 6-14.) A clear-plastic template works well because you can see the grain of the wood through it. (See Illus. 6-15.) Templates are also useful for laying out objects on the workpiece. This minimizes waste. (See Illus. 6-16.)

Templates are useful on some large workpieces where part of the pattern can be drawn on opposite sides of the workpiece.

Illus. 6-14. *A solid template is used to trace a pattern directly onto the workpiece.*

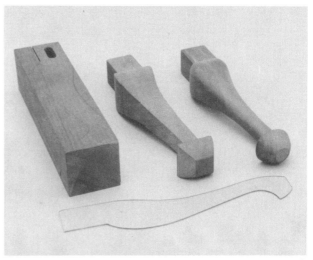

Illus. 6-15. *This cabriole leg was traced with a clear-plastic template.*

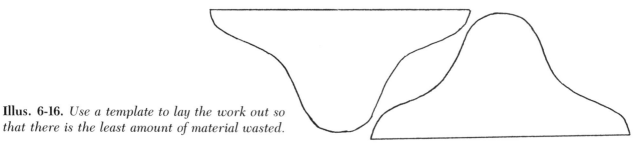

Illus. 6-16. *Use a template to lay the work out so that there is the least amount of material wasted.*

Pattern Sawing

Pattern sawing is a technique used to make multiple pieces that are identical. A solid pattern is attached to the workpiece. It works best if the pattern is made of plywood, because plywood, unlike solid wood, is stable (does not shrink or expand).

To pattern-saw, do the following:

1. Clamp a rub block to the saw table. (See Illus. 6-17.) The rub block should have a curved end with a notch in it. The notch fits over the blade, extending past it about 1/16 inch. (See Illus. 6-18.) Cut out the rub block so that the workpiece can slide underneath it.

Illus. 6-17. *Clamp the rub block to the table.*

Illus. 6-18. *The notch in the rub block fits over the blade and protrudes past it about ⅟₁₆ inch.*

2. Tape the plywood pattern to the workpiece with double-face tape. (See Illus. 6-19 and 6-20.) The pattern will contact the rub block during the cut.

3. Because the blade is about ⅟₁₆ inch short of the pattern, the workpiece extends past the pattern about ⅟₁₆ inch. (See Illus. 6-21–6-23.)

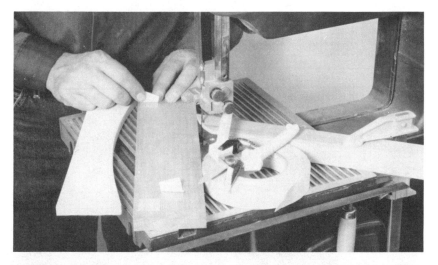

Illus. 6-19. *Use double-face tape to attach the template to the workpiece.*

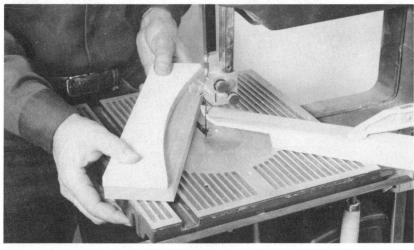

Illus. 6-20. *Press the template firmly onto the tape. Be careful not to use too much tape or it will be difficult to get the template off.*

Illus. 6-21. *Begin the cut with the template touching the rub block.*

Illus. 6-22. *As you continue cutting, use slight pressure to keep the template against the rub block.*

Illus. 6-23. *The completed cut. The workpiece should extend about ⅟₁₆ inch past the pattern.*

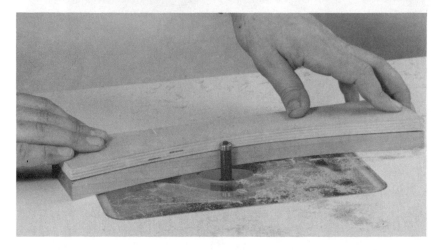

Illus. 6-24. *While the template is still attached to the pattern, trim off the waste with a router. The router bit being used for this operation is called a flush-cutting bit. The bearing on top of the bit rides against the pattern.*

4. Trim away the ¹⁄₁₆-inch waste with a router table and a "flush-cutting" router bit. A flush-cutting router bit is a bit with a bearing on top of it. The bearing rubs against the pattern as the cutter trims the waste. (See Illus. 6-24.) The finish is smooth and requires little sanding.

Pattern-sawing is easy. This technique is particularly useful for projects that have a number of pieces that are exactly the same size with multiple curves. The stacking office-shelves shown in Illus. 6-25 were easily and efficiently pattern-sawed. This technique was also used to make the curved edge on the turned plate shown in Illus. 6-26, and the door panel shown in 6-27.

Illus. 6-25. *These stacking paper trays were made using the pattern-sawing technique.*

Illus. 6-26. *The plate on the right was turned, and then its edge was pattern-routed using the plywood template on the left.*

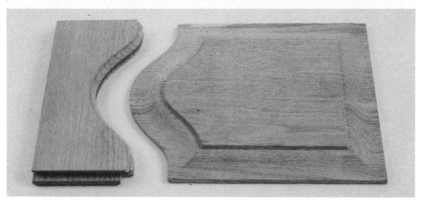

Illus. 6-27. *Both these top and bottom pieces of a door were made using the pattern-routing technique.*

Chapter 7

SCROLL SAWING

In the past, a special piece of equipment called a scroll saw was used with narrow blades to make tight turns. This procedure was called scroll-sawing.

Today, with the introduction of Cool Blocks (nonmetallic guide blocks) and ⅟₁₆-inch blades, it is possible to do scroll-saw work with a band saw.

In fact, in some instances it is very hard to tell the difference between work done with a band saw and that done with an expensive scroll saw.

A ⅟₁₆-inch band-saw blade has a very fine pitch (many teeth per inch), so that the final cut will be smooth. It can make very accurate straight cuts. Illus. 7-1 shows a straight cut made in oak with a

Illus. 7-1. *A ⅟₁₆-inch-wide band-saw blade can also be used to make extremely straight cuts. A cut this straight would be difficult if not impossible with a scroll saw.*

Illus. 7-2. *The letters shown here are the smallest-size letters that are practical to cut with the band saw. The pencil gives scale to the size of the letters and the blade.*

⅟₁₆-inch band-saw blade. A cut this straight would be extremely hard, if not impossible, to do with a scroll saw.

Narrow band-saw blades can also be used to make cuts in thick material. This can be useful when the band saw is used to make name signs. (See Illus. 7-2.)

Making Inside Cuts with a Narrow Blade

You can use a narrow blade on a band saw to make inside cuts. To do this, cut two halves of the piece, and then glue them together. We will refer to this technique as the "cut and glue" technique. The items shown in Illus. 7-3 were made with this technique. The design on the pencil holder is a "negative space." This means that the design was created when its area was cut out.

The cut and glue technique has several advantages. Both sides of the pattern are cut at the same time, which means that you save time sawing. (See Illus. 7-4–7-8.) The more complex the pattern, the greater the savings in time. Also, because the two sides are cut at the same time, they are perfectly symmetrical. This improves the quality of the cut. This is very important because no matter how good you are at scroll-sawing, it is extremely difficult to make two halves of a pattern exactly the same.

The time it takes to glue the pieces together is minimal when compared to the time it would take to cut the two halves individually. Gluing may require some creative techniques. Dowels help to locate the two halves in relation to each other. Clothespins were used to clamp the two interior halves together on the bookcase and the letter holder shown in Illus. 7-3.

Illus. 7-3. *The cut and glue technique was used to create the cut-out patterns for the adjustable book shelf, pencil holder, and letter holder shown here.*

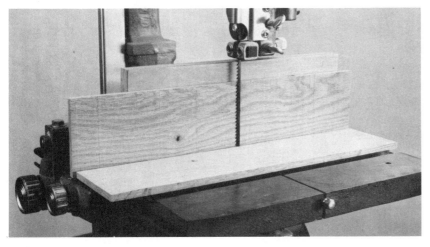

Illus. 7-4. *Although you can use the cut and glue technique with any two boards, the finished item will look better if you cut the pieces from the same board and glue them back together. Cutting the board into two pieces on edge is called **resawing**. Gluing the re-sawed pieces back together is called **bookmatching**. These techniques are discussed in Chapter 10.*

Illus. 7-5. *After you have cut the pieces, use double-face tape to hold them together.*

Illus. 7-6. *Use rubber cement to attach the pattern to the pieces. Note that turning holes are being used here. They will make it easier for the operator to cut the pattern.*

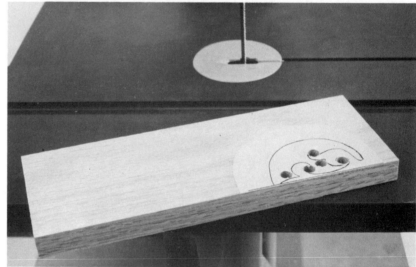

Illus. 7-7. *Remove the large piece of waste. Here a ⅛-inch-wide blade is being used.*

Illus. 7-8. *The completed two halves of the piece. Remove the pattern, and glue the pieces together. A clothespin makes a good clamp for the two narrow pieces inside the pattern.*

Chapter 8
MAKING CURVES

One advantage the band saw has over other power tools is that it can cut curves in both thick and thin wood. A curved cut is possible because the workpiece can be rotated around the narrow blade. (See Illus. 8-1.) When the workpiece is turned sharply, the back of the blade rubs against the saw kerf. (See Illus. 8-2.) This is the smallest turn that it is possible to make. If you rotate the workpiece past this point, the blade body will start to twist. This should be avoided if possible because twisting the blade shortens its life. To prevent the blade from twisting, make sure that you feed the workpiece forward into the blade during a sharp turn, and that you use a blade of the appropriate width. Refer to the blade-width chart on page 24 if you are not sure of the blade width.

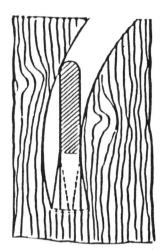

Illus. 8-2. During a sharp turn, the back of the blade rubs against the kerf. Do not try to make a tighter turn at this point. It will twist the blade. Always try to avoid twisting the blade.

Illus. 8-1. When making a curved cut, slowly rotate the workpiece. As the cut progresses, slowly move your hands to the back of the workpiece. Use your thumb to move the piece forward.

It is important that you plan ahead when making turns. Planning helps to minimize the wasted material and decrease the difficulty of the cut. For example, when making a piece that has parallel curves, it is possible to make one curved cut and then glue the two separate pieces back together with their flat sides in contact with each other. (See Illus. 8-3.) This saves time and material, and increases the accuracy of the cut. If you choose the grain carefully, the glue line will be nearly impossible to see.

ONE PIECE CUT LIKE THIS

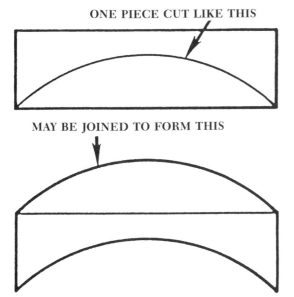

MAY BE JOINED TO FORM THIS

Illus. 8-3. In this technique, the cut pieces are glued, and form a curved piece with parallel sides.

When cutting multiple pieces with parallel curves, it is possible to use the rip fence to space the width of the workpiece. (See Illus. 8-4.) A rip fence is an accessory used to control the saw when a cut is being made along the grain of the wood. The workpiece should be touching the fence about ¼ inch in front of the saw blade. (See Illus. 8-5 and 8-6.) This technique allows you to make multiple pieces that are exactly the same size with very little effort. It works on small and large workpieces, and was used to make the knockdown lawn chair shown in Illus. 8-7.

Using the Single-Point Technique for Curves

As just discussed, the rip fence can be used as a rotation point for determining the width of the workpiece. This technique works well if the piece is a gentle curve in one direction. If the piece curves in several directions a similar technique is used, except that the rotation point is a pointed stick rather than the rip fence. Clamp the pointed stick to the fence or the table. (See Illus. 8-8.) If the curve to be cut is a gentle curve, use a stick with a rounded point. Hold the

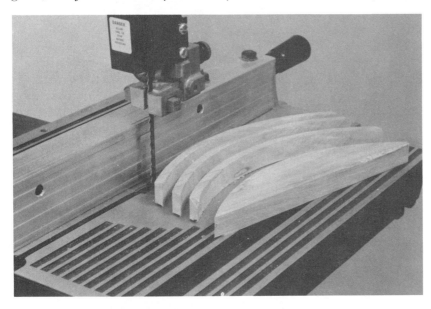

Illus. 8-4. It is easy to cut multiple pieces with parallel curves if you use the rip fence to space the width of the workpiece.

Illus. 8-5. *It is best to contact the fence with the workpiece slightly in front of the blade. This is the pivot point.*

Illus. 8-6. *The distance between the blade and the fence determines the width of the workpiece. Keep the workpiece against the fence while making the cut.*

Illus. 8-7. *This knockdown chair was made with the parallel-curve technique.*

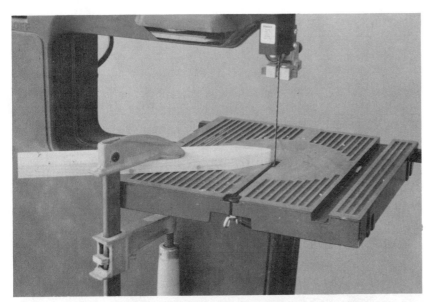

Illus. 8-8. *A single-point technique is used to do a variety of work. The rotation point is simply a stick with a round point clamped to the table.*

Illus. 8-9. *To use the single-point technique, place the tip of the point, as indicated by the pencil tip, about ⅛ inch in front of the blade.*

Illus. 8-10. *The workpiece contacts the point before the blade.*

edge of the workpiece against the point. (See Illus. 8-9 and 8-10.) You have to "fish tail" or angle the piece into the blade at the correct angle.

This technique does require some skill and concentration. (See Illus. 8-11–8-15.) It is particularly useful on pieces with multiple curves, such as chair backs. (See Illus. 8-16.) It is also useful on small objects with multiple curves, such as band-sawed boxes. (See Illus. 8-17.) When the single-point technique is used for small objects or tight curves, the point on the stick should be sharp rather than rounded. For a box like the one shown in Illus. 8-17, use a ⅛-inch blade with a sharp rotation point about ⅛ inch in front of it.

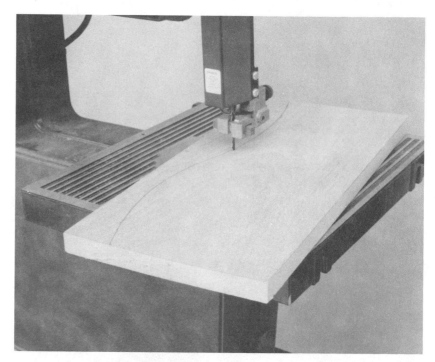

Illus. 8-11. *To make multiple curves with the single-point technique, make the first cut in the usual manner.*

Illus. 8-12. *Complete the first cut. Make it as smooth as possible.*

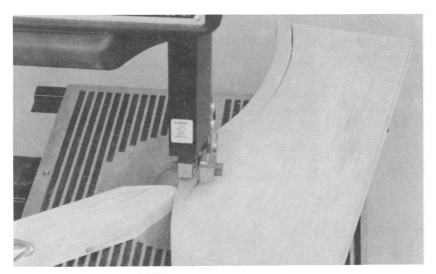

Illus. 8-13. *Start the cut with the corner against the point of the stick. Continue the cut by putting light pressure against the point. It is not enough to just hold the piece against the point and shove. You have to move the workpiece back and forth (called fishtailing).*

Illus. 8-14. *The completed first piece.*

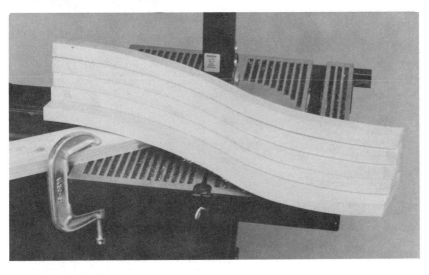

Illus. 8-15. *Multiple pieces that are exactly the same can be made with this technique.*

Illus. 8-16. *This technique is particularly useful on pieces with multiple curves, such as chair backs.*

Illus. 8-17. *The single-point technique was used to make the inside curve of this band-sawn box. To make curves like the ones on this box, make sure that you use a stick with a sharp point. (Photo courtesy of Barbara Reifscheider, Colchester, CT)*

Chapter 9

CIRCULAR WORK

Many projects require either complete circles or a portion of a circle. Although it is possible to cut a circle freehand, this is not the most accurate way. The most accurate way would be to use a circle-cutting jig.

Circle-cutting jigs are commercially available or can be shop-made. Commercially available jigs and shop-made jigs work the same way. The work is rotated around a screw or nail similar to the way a compass rotates around a central point. This screw or nail—the rotation point—should be even with the front of the blade.

The rotation point is held in place by the jig. The rotation point can be either above the workpiece or below it. Having the rotation point on the bottom is more accurate than having it on top.

Illus. 9-1–9-3 show a shop-made plywood jig with a rotation point mounted on the bottom. The rotation point is simply a sharpened nail located on a pencil line that is even with the front of the blade. The jig consists of a solid piece of wood that fits in the mitre slot. It is attached to the bottom of the plywood platform. The jig slides in the mitre slot. Its forward motion is stopped by a piece of wood clamped to the wooden mitre bar. (See Illus. 9-2.)

This circle-cutting jig is easy to make. Simply do the following:

1. Use two pieces of wood for the jig. One piece should be a piece of plywood about 16 inches square. The other should be a solid piece of wood the size of the mitre slot.

2. Before nailing the strip to the bottom of the plywood, cut about two inches off the end. This will later be clamped to the strip and used as a stop. (See Illus. 9-2.)

3. After the pieces are nailed together, with the blade running advance the piece of plywood into the blade until it is cut halfway across.

4. Turn off the saw and make a pencil mark 90° to the saw cut. The rotation point is located on this pencil line.

5. Adjust the stop so that the front tip of the tooth touches the pencil line. Use a nail or screw as the rotation point (See Illus. 9-4–9-6). The radius of the circle is the distance between the blade and the rotation point.

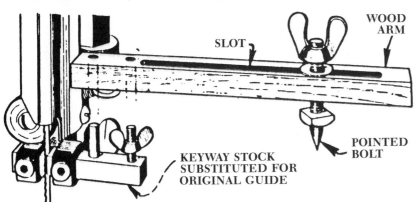

SLOT

WOOD ARM

KEYWAY STOCK SUBSTITUTED FOR ORIGINAL GUIDE

POINTED BOLT

Illus. 9-1. *This shop-made rotation point is mounted on top of the workpiece.*

Illus. 9-2. *A shop-made circle-cutting jig that is made of plywood. A piece of scrap wood is clamped to the mitre guide piece. This creates a stop. The stop should stop the jig when the rotation point is 90 degrees to the front of the saw blade.*

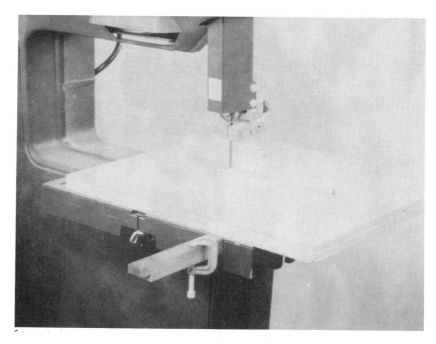

Illus. 9-3. *A side view of the plywood circle-cutting jig.*

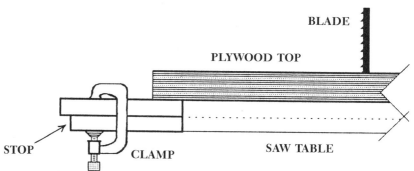

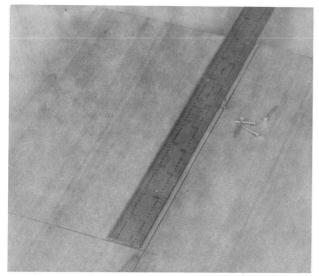

Illus. 9-4. *Measure the desired radius with a ruler and place a nail at that point.*

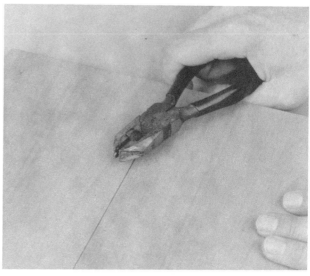

Illus. 9-5. *Cut off the head of the nail with a pair of pliers.*

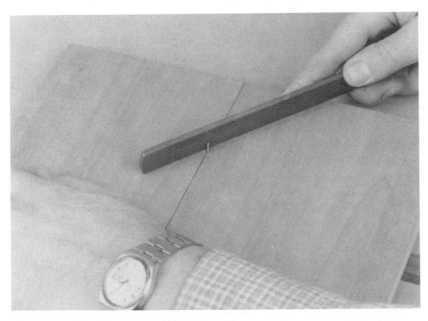

Illus. 9-6. *File the nail to a point. This nail is the rotation point.*

To use the jig, do the following:

1. Puncture a small hole into the center of the workpiece and mount the workpiece onto the point.

2. Move the jig and the workpiece into the blade until the stop touches the table. The stop has to stay in contact with the table or the cut will not be round.

3. Slowly rotate the workpiece on the point until the circle is completed. (See Illus. 9-7–9-9.)

If you angle the table, the circle that you cut will be wider at the top than at the bottom. This is useful when you are cutting thick circles to be used for bowl blanks. You will be able to make more accurate bowl blanks if you use the jig. (See Illus. 9-10.)

Illus. 9-7. *Advance the workpiece into the blade.*

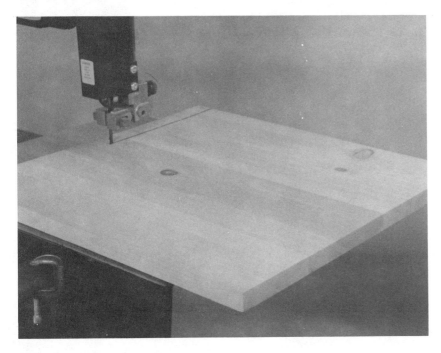

Illus. 9-8. *Rotate the workpiece. Make sure that the stop is against the table. Rotating the piece can cause the jig to move rearwards.*

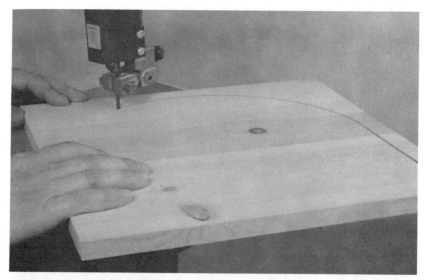

Illus. 9-9. *A perfect circle that was cut with the shop-made jig.*

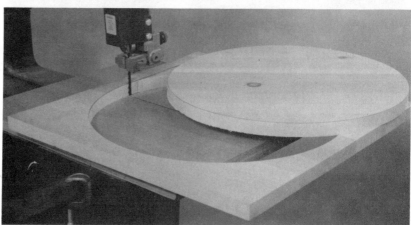

Illus. 9-10. *If you angle the band-saw table, the piece will be wider at the top than at the bottom, which is useful when you are turning bowls. (Drawing courtesy of INCA of Switzerland)*

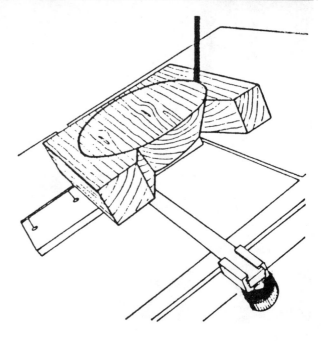

Half-Circle Jig

Many projects require partial circles. The circle-cutting jig just described can be used to make these cuts. Rather than advancing the jig and the workpiece into the blade, clamp the circle-cutting jig to the table and only rotate the workpiece into the blade.

Another way to cut a partial circle is to make a jig that holds the workpiece, and then rotate the jig and the workpiece together. Illus. 9-11 and 9-12 show such a jig: one used to cut half-circles. This jig is a piece of plywood with a rotation point on the bottom of it. Two plywood sides are added to stabilize the workpiece. A clamp is used to hold the workpiece in place during the saw cut. (See Illus. 9-13.)

This jig was used to make the half-circle cuts for the letter holder and the knockdown bookshelf shown in Illus. 9-14. This half-circle jig and the quarter-circle jig described in the following section are made the same way.

Illus. 9-11. *The half-circle jig rests on top of the circle-cutting jig. The circle-cutting jig, a commercial jig that is manufactured by INCA, cannot be shown here. The cut shown here is half completed.*

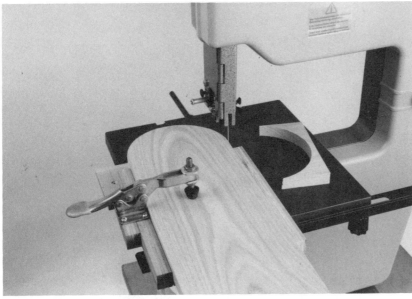

Illus. 9-12. *The completed cut with the half-circle jig.*

Illus. 9-13. *The half-circle jig consists of a piece of plywood with strips of plywood nailed to its sides. An adjustable clamp is used to hold the workpiece during the saw cut.*

Illus. 9-14. *The half-circle jig was used to make the cuts in the bookcase and the letter holder. The jig is particularly useful for pieces like the bookshelf, in which the center is hollow.*

Making the Half-Circle Jig

To make the half-circle jig, do the following:

1. Cut a piece of plywood the diameter of the circle.

2. Make a hole for the rotation point. The hole should be half the width of the plywood (which is the radius of the circle).

3. Using the rotation point, make a half-circle cut in the plywood.

4. Attach two sides to the plywood base. This will keep the workpieces stable during the cuts. You can also add a clamp to secure the workpiece to the jig.

Quarter-Circle Jig

To make a quarter-circle jig, do the following:

1. Determine the radius of the partial circle.

2. Measure the distance from each edge of the workpiece to the rotation point.

3. Locate the rotation point and cut the corner off. (See Illus. 9-15.)

4. Add two pieces of wood to the side.

5. Rotate the workpiece and the jig into the blade.

6. Cut the corner. You do not have to measure, mark, or make a puncture hole. (See Illus. 9-16 and 9-17.)

A quarter-circle jig was used to round off the corners of the bottom and back of the knockdown bookshelf shown in Illus. 9-18.

Illus. 9-15. *Locate the rotation point.*

Illus. 9-16. *The piece is rotated into the saw blade, making a quarter-circle cut.*

Illus. 9-17. *You can make the cut without having to measure, mark, or make a hole.*

Illus. 9-18. *The quarter-circle jig was used to cut the corners on the back and the bottom of the knockdown bookshelf. This quarter-circle jig can also be used with a narrow belt sander to finish the edge.*

Off-Center Rotation Points

Off-center rotation points can be used to create some very interesting designs for projects. An off-center rotation point was used to create the designs for the chair parts shown in 9-19. You can make cuts easily and accurately with off-center rotation points if you use the circle-cutting jigs just described.

There are different types of off-center rotation point. One off-center rotation point, called a corner rotation point, is used to remove a quarter-circle of waste. In this case, the rotation point is between the column and the blade. Because the location of the rotation point is on that part of the workpiece that will be waste material, you can drill a small hole in the corner and nail the workpiece to the jig. (See Illus. 9-20.) This technique is used to make the cuts for the Shaker step stool shown in Illus. 9-22.

It is often easier to cut the quarter-circles when making a half-circle before gluing the pieces together. Using the rotation point opposite the column doesn't work in some situations because the workpiece would rotate into the column.

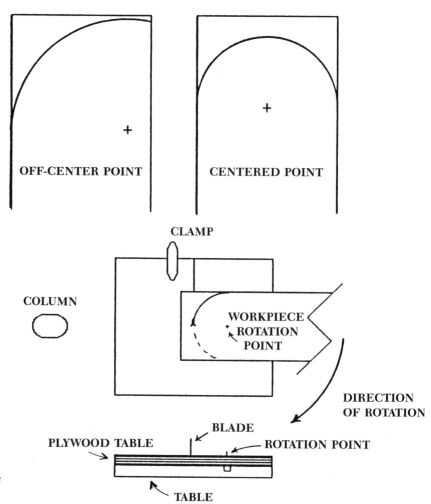

OFF-CENTER POINT

CENTERED POINT

CLAMP

COLUMN

WORKPIECE

ROTATION POINT

DIRECTION OF ROTATION

BLADE

PLYWOOD TABLE

ROTATION POINT

TABLE

Illus. 9-19. The chair parts shown above can be created with various off-center rotation points.

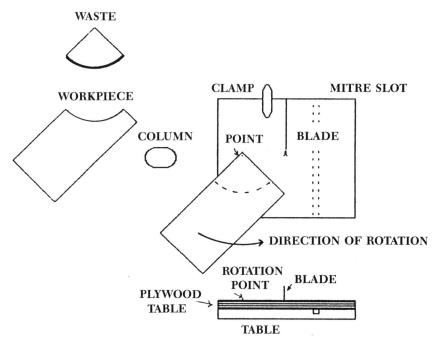

WASTE

WORKPIECE

COLUMN

CLAMP

MITRE SLOT

POINT

BLADE

DIRECTION OF ROTATION

ROTATION POINT

BLADE

PLYWOOD TABLE

TABLE

FRONT VIEW

Illus. 9-20. *To remove a round corner, use a rotation point that is between the blade and the saw column. Make an auxiliary wood table that mounts on the top of the saw table. Drill a hole in the corner of the workpiece and use a nail as the rotation point.*

Illus. 9-21. *Cut the quarter circle before gluing the front and back together. This quarter-circle cut is being made for the Shaker step stool shown in Illus. 9-22.*

Illus. 9-22. *The completed Shaker step stool.*

Chapter 10

MAKING STRAIGHT CUTS

The band saw is useful for making straight cuts. In fact, it is often used to rip small pieces of wood because it is much safer than either a radial arm saw or a table saw. Because the force of the cut is straight down on the table, the work cannot be pulled away or kicked back, which sometimes happens with table or radial arm saws.

The band saw can also cut thicker stock than the radial arm or table saw, and is therefore often used to make straight cuts in thick material. The one disadvantage of cutting with the band saw is that the saw cut is not as smooth as that made by a table or radial arm saw. However, most of the time the band-sawed edge can be either planed or jointed straight and smooth.

There are two techniques for making straight band saw cuts. One technique is to feed the work into the blade freehand. (See Illus. 10-1.) The other technique is to use a jig or fixture to control the workpiece. To maintain consistency and accuracy, you should use a jig or fixture, if possible.

The fixtures most often used are the mitre gauge, the rip fence, and the tap jig. In special situations, a fixture that slides in the mitre slot is used. These specialty fixtures are beyond the scope of this book, but are covered in detail in *Band Saw Handbook*, which is also published by Sterling Publishing Company.

Crosscutting

A crosscut is a cut made across (against) the grain of the workpiece. A mitre gauge is the fixture that is commonly used when a band saw is being

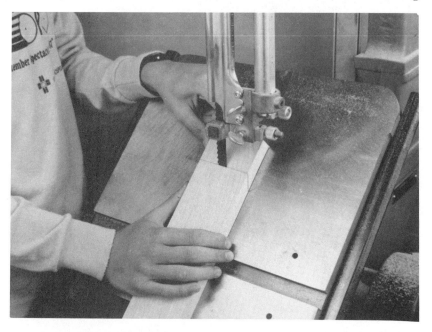

Illus. 10-1. *This bevel cut is being made freehand. A wide blade with a fine pitch is the best type of blade to use to crosscut.*

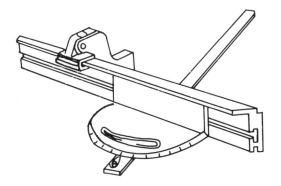

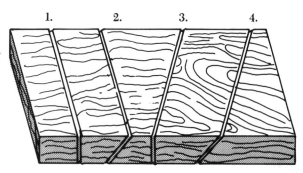

1. CROSSCUT
2. BEVELLED CROSSCUT
3. MITRE CUT
4. COMPOUND
   MITRE CUT

used to crosscut. (See Illus. 10-2.) The head of the mitre gauge adjusts to the desired angle of the cut. The standard crosscut is made with the mitre gauge set at 90 degrees. (See Illus. 10-3.) A bevel crosscut is made with the mitre gauge at 90 degrees and the table angled. A mitre cut is made with the table at 90 degrees and with the mitre gauge angled. A compound mitre cut is made with both the mitre gauge and the table angled. (See Illus. 10-4 and 10-5.)

A rip fence can also be used to make straight crosscuts. It is particularly useful on wide boards. (See Illus. 10-6.) A squaring jig can be used in conjunction with the rip fence to make an accurate crosscut. A squaring jig is a square piece of plywood with a knob or handle in the middle of it. The workpiece is held against the squaring jig, and the adjacent side of the jig is held against the fence. The jig and the workpiece are moved into the blade as a unit. (See Illus. 10-7.)

Illus. 10-3. *This crosscut is being made with a mitre guide.*

Illus. 10-4. *The operator is cutting this mitre by using the mitre gauge in an angled position. The work is clamped to prevent the wood from slipping during the cut.*

Illus. 10-5. *A compound angle cut is made with both the table and the mitre gauge angled.*

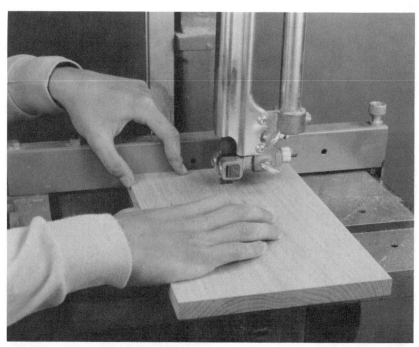

Illus. 10-6. *The rip fence is useful for crosscutting wide stock.*

Illus. 10-7. *This squaring jig, with a plane-type handle, is being used with the rip fence to make an accurate crosscut.*

If you are going to make a lot of straight crosscuts, it is recommended that you use a narrow blade with standard teeth. A wide blade usually works best for straight cuts, but wide blades usually have skip or hook teeth, which are not the best choice for crosscutting. You can order wide blades with standard teeth, but it is easier to use a narrow blade with standard teeth.

Use a blade with a pitch of 12 to 14 teeth per inch. This type of blade works best for crosscutting. One-eighth-inch blades usually have a pitch of 12 to 14 teeth per inch. Because narrow blades flex rearwards during the cut, they make very accurate cuts. (See Illus. 10-8 and 10-9.)

You can increase the accuracy of narrow blades such as ⅛-inch and ⅟₁₆-inch blades if you raise the guide about an inch above the work. This allows the blade to flex backwards in a gentle arc, which exposes the blade under the guide. But *be forewarned:* Raising the guide can be dangerous, so be very careful. Cool Blocks, which are nonmetallic replacement guide blocks, can be used in contact with the blade and increase the accuracy of the cut.

Illus. 10-8. *A ⅟₁₆-inch-wide blade flexes rearward during the cut. This results in a very accurate cut. Narrow blades last long if the guide is kept about an inch above the work. But be forewarned: When the guide is raised above the work, the blade is exposed. This can be dangerous, so be careful.*

Illus. 10-9. *Here a ⅛-inch-wide blade is being used to free small dowels.*

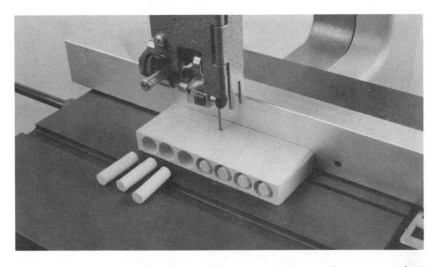

Ripping

Ripping is a cut made with the grain of the wood. The three most common cuts made with the grain are rip, bevel, and resaw cuts. (See Illus. 10-10.)

Two techniques are commonly used to make straight rip cuts. One technique is to use the rip fence as a guide. Another technique is to use a single point to guide the work. (See Illus. 10-11 and 10-12.)

The rationale for using the single point is that the saw may tend to cut at a slight angle. This is often called "lead". The single point allows the operator to feed the wood into the blade at a slight angle, which compensates for blade lead. With a little practice, you will get satisfactory results with the single-point method.

If you are going to make a lot of rip cuts, it is best to adjust the angle of the rip fence to correspond with blade lead. This is a fairly simple procedure that will only take a minute. Do the following:

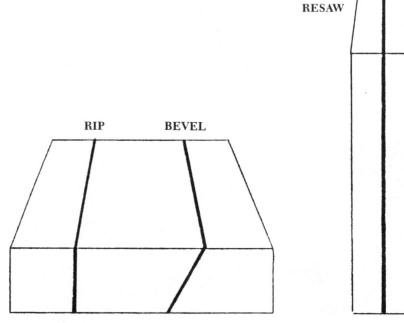

Illus. 10-10. *The three most common cuts made with the grain are rip, bevel, and resaw cuts.*

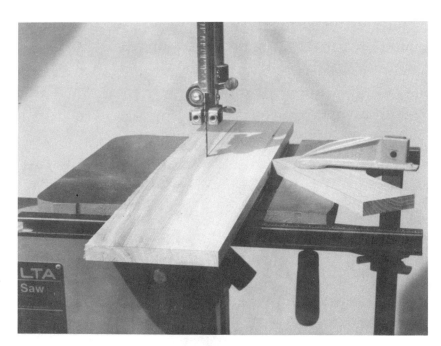

Illus. 10-11. *The single-point method allows the wood to be fed into the blade at a slight angle. This angle compensates for blade lead.*

Illus. 10-12. *This square piece of wood clamped to the table functions as a single-point resaw fence.*

1. Make a straight pencil mark on the edge of the board. (See Illus. 10-13.)

2. Feed the wood into the blade. Cut next to the pencil mark. (See Illus. 10-14.) If the blade is leading, you will have to angle it slightly to keep it cutting along the pencil mark.

3. Stop the cut in the middle of the board and mark the angle on the table with a pencil. (See Illus. 10-15.) This is the angle at which the blade

is leading, and thus it is the best angle at which to feed work into the blade.

4. Loosen the bolts which hold the rip fence, and adjust the angle of the fence to correspond with the mark on the table. (See Illus. 10-16.)

Each time you change the blade when you plan on ripping, it is a good idea to adjust the angle of the fence.

Illus. 10-13. *To test the blade, mark the wood with a straight pencil mark. Feed the wood into the blade so that it follows the pencil mark.*

Illus. 10-14. *Feed the wood into the blade on the pencil mark.*

Illus. 10-15. *To make a straight cut, you may have to angle the workpiece slightly. Mark the angle. This is the angle at which the saw blade cuts best.*

Illus. 10-16. *Loosen the fence bolts with a wrench, and change the angle of the fence so that it corresponds to the angle of the test cut.*

Making a Rip Fence

On most band saws, the rip fence is an optional piece of equipment that you can buy. On older saws, you may not have the option of buying a fence because it may not be available. You can make your own rip fence adjustable for blade lead with two pieces of plywood. (See Illus. 10-17 and 10-18.) Attach a piece of sandpaper to the top of the small piece of plywood. This will prevent the two pieces from rotating in relationship to one another. Clamp the shop-made fence to the front of the table. You can add a wide piece of wood to the fence if you want a higher fence for tasks such as resawing.

Resawing

Resawing is the process of cutting a board in half along its width. (See Illus. 10-19.) It is a good idea to add an extension fence to the rip fence when you plan to resaw. The extension fence will help support the workpiece. (See Illus. 10-20.) Check to ensure that the table is square to the blade, and that the fence is square to the table. If the blade and the fence are both square to the table, they should be parallel with each other.

When the board is resawed and the two pieces are lying flat, next to each other, you will note that they are mirror images of each other. When

Illus. 10-17. *The fence is held in place with a clamp.*

Illus. 10-18. *Attaching a piece of sandpaper to the top of the small piece of plywood will prevent the two pieces from rotating in relationship with each other.*

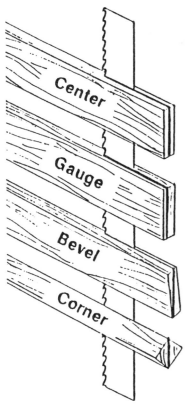

Illus. 10-19. *Resawing is cutting a board in half along its width.*

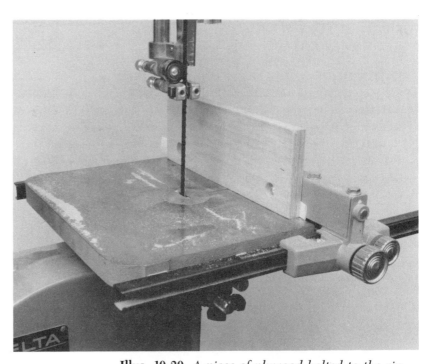

Illus. 10-20. *A piece of plywood bolted to the rip fence extends to the height of the fence. A paper shim between the plywood and the fence keeps the fence square.*

Illus. 10-21. *Resawing exposes the two inside surfaces of the board. The two surfaces are mirror images of each other. When the two matching halves are glued together, it is called bookmatching.*

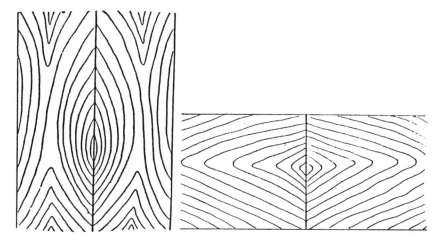

Illus. **10-22.** *On the left are two boards that were bookmatched side to side. On the right are two boards that were bookmatched end to end. End-to-end bookmatching is only used for veneer because solid-wood end grain does not make a good gluing surface.*

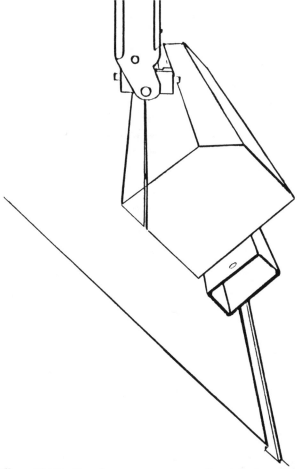

Illus. 10-23. *Bevel cuts are cuts made with the table tilted. The rip fence helps to feed the wood straight and to keep it from sliding off the table.*

these two boards are glued together, it is called "bookmatching." (See Illus. 10-21 and 10-22.)

Bookmatching greatly enhances the character of a piece and is useful on all surfaces that are flat, such as tabletops and doors.

Bevel Cuts

Bevel cuts are made with the table tilted. It is best to use the rip fence on the downhill side of the blade so that the workpiece cannot slide off the table. (See Illus. 10-23.) It is also possible to use a V-block to support the workpiece rather than tilting the table.

Cutting Round Stock

When cutting round stock, it is important that you make the cut through the middle of the workpiece. If the cut is located anywhere but the middle of the board, the downward pressure from the blade will cause the piece to rotate. This rotation often breaks the blade. A V-block can be used to support the workpiece during the cut. (See Illus. 10-24.)

Tapers

Tapers are angled cuts made along the grain of the workpiece. (See Illus. 10-25.) You can cut

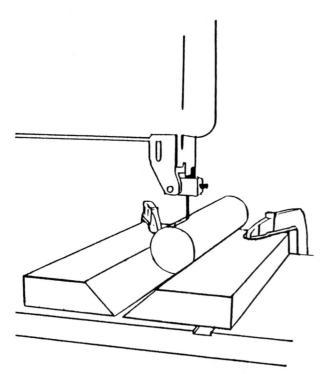

Illus. 10-24. *Round stock should only be cut through its center. A V-block can be used to support the workpiece during the cut.*

short tapers using a mitre gauge. (See Illus. 10-26.) When making tapered cuts on a long piece, use a jig. You can make your own.

Taper jigs come in three varieties. The simplest one is the *fixed-angle jig*. (See Illus. 10-27.) The *step jig* is used to make a taper on one side, opposite sides, or adjacent sides of a workpiece. A step jig, as the name implies, is a fixture using three notches or steps. The jig rides against the rip fence of the saw. The first cut is made with the workpiece resting on the middle or second step. To make a taper on the opposite side of the workpiece, use the third step on the jig. (See Illus. 10-28.) To make a taper on the adjacent side, rotate the workpiece 90 degrees.

The step jig is easy to make. Machine a piece of wood the width of the desired taper. Cut three pieces off the end and glue them, creating the steps about ¼ inch high.

The *adjustable taper jig* has a hinge on one end and a locking mechanism on the opposite end. This jig can be adjusted to the desired angle. Illus. 10-30 shows a commercial version of the jig, but it is easy to make one out of scrap wood.

Illus. 10-25. *Shown here are the three types of tapered cuts.*

| | ONE-SIDED CUT | TWO-SIDED CUT | FOUR-SIDED CUT |

Illus. 10-26. *The mitre gauge can be used if the tapers are not too long.*

Illus. 10-27. *A fixed-angle jig is simply an angled piece of wood with a brass screw in the end.*

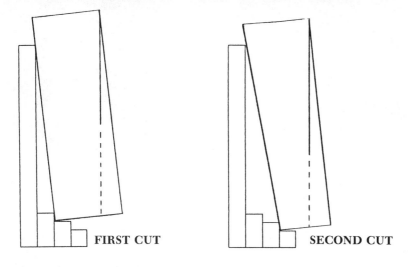

FIRST CUT **SECOND CUT**

Illus. 10-28. *The step jig is used for opposite or adjacent side tapers. To make tapers on opposite sides, use the second step for the first cut (shown on the left). To make the second cut, flip the piece over and make the cut on the third step.*

Illus. 10-29. *To make tapers on adjacent sides using the taper jig, use the second step for both cuts. After the first cut, rotate the piece 90 degrees for the second cut.*

Illus. 10-30. *This commercially available jig is adjustable. It has a taper of one inch per foot.*

Chapter 11

DECORATIVE CUTTING TECHNIQUES

The band saw can be used for a wide range of creative techniques. In fact, it is sometimes argued that it is limited only by the imagination of the user. Now that you have learned basic straight and curve cuts, you should learn some of these decorative cutting techniques. It is hoped that the techniques discussed here will encourage you to experiment with others.

Sawing Multicolored Layers

One very simple technique is to cut a stack of boards of different colors, and then glue the boards back together alternating the colors. If you stack three different-colored boards, and

Illus. 11-1. *These pieces are being held together with double-faced tape. The cuts were made with a ½-inch hook-tooth blade with a pitch of 3 TPI.*

Illus. 11-2. *Separate the pieces from each other and then glue them together.*

then make two saw cuts, you will have three cut boards that have a similar design but vary in color. (See Illus. 11-1 and 11-2.)

Hold the pieces together with narrow strips of double-faced tape. Use a ½-inch hook-tooth blade with a pitch of 3 TPI to make the cuts. After the cuts are made, gently sand the surface to remove any roughness. However, be careful not to remove too much material or the pieces will not fit tightly. Also be careful not to round the corners.

Puzzles

It is easy to make puzzles if you use a narrow blade such as a ¹⁄₁₆-inch-wide blade. The bear puzzle shown in Illus. 11-3 is from *Scroll Saw Pattern Book*, by Pat and Patricia Spielman. The material used is ¾-inch-thick clear pine. You can use the same blade on a band saw to cut much thicker material—up to three inches thick. You can also rotate the piece 90 degrees, and then make cuts from an adjacent side.

Making Multiple Pieces

At times, you may want to make more than one particular item. Obviously, the more items that you cut at a time, the less time it takes to make each item, on an average. There are two basic techniques for making multiple pieces. One is called slicing. The other is called stack-sawing. Both are examined below.

Slicing

"Slicing" is the technique of cutting individual thin pieces off the end of a large piece. The numeral "2" piece shown in Illus. 11-4 was cut out of a solid block of wood. Its edges were sanded before the slicing cuts were made.

If you want a smooth finish on the face (sawed surface) of the workpiece, sand the piece *before* cutting it off. This can be done by hand or by machine. The machine-sanding technique is described on pages 114–116.

Illus. 11-3. This puzzle was cut with a ¹⁄₁₆-inch-wide blade. The design for the puzzle is from the Scroll Saw Pattern Book, *by Pat and Patricia Spielman, published by Sterling Publishing Company.*

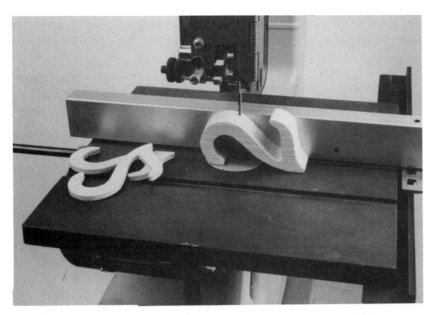

Illus. 11-4. *Slicing is the technique of cutting small pieces from one larger piece.*

The number "2" shown in Illus. 11-4 does not need a smooth surface. However, if you wanted to sand a smooth surface on each individual part, you would have to rotate the piece 180 degrees so that you can cut it from the bottom rather than the top, as is shown in Illus. 11-4. This would leave the smooth surface on the appropriate side.

One disadvantage of slicing is that it requires thick stock, which can be expensive. Also, this technique of cutting thick pieces into small ones can be a wasteful one in some situations. However, it is a good technique when you are cutting objects out of inexpensive wood.

Stack Sawing

Stack sawing, as the name implies, is the technique of stacking pieces together, and then cutting them. This makes the cutting process very efficient because a number of pieces are cut at once. To ensure that the cut will be accurate and consistent, make sure that the layers of material are held together with nails, screws, jigs, or glue. Padding compound and hot-melt glue seem to work best. Padding compound is a rubberized liquid that dries in a couple of minutes. It is used to make paper pads. It creates a solid block of

Illus. 11-5. *This stack of plywood is held together with padding compound, which is a rubberized liquid used to hold paper tablets together.*

material similar to a wood tablet that can be cut with the saw. (See Illus. 11-5.) You can get padding compound from office suppliers or from printing businesses.

Illus. 11-6 shows an example of stack sawing in which 12 pieces of plywood are being cut at one time. The pieces are held together with hot-melt glue. A ⅛-inch-wide blade is used because it will cut the fine detail. It has a 14 TPI pitch because this ensures that it will give a smooth cut. The 12 pieces that are being cut will form two snowflake designs. Each design will feature six of the pieces. (See Illus. 11-7.) When gluing the pieces together, glue three individual pieces at a time, and then glue them into the complete unit. (See Illus. 11-8.)

Illus. 11-6. *These 12 pieces of plywood are held together by hot-melt glue applied to the waste area. (Hot melt glue is a type of glue that is applied hot. It forms a bond when it cools.) The pieces will be freed when the last piece of waste is cut away.*

Illus. 11-7. *Six pieces form the snowflake design.*

Illus. 11-8. *The completed snowflake. This is a project in the next chapter.*

Making Decorative Boxes

Making boxes with a band saw is fun. Illus. 11-9 shows three different types of box. The shell-shaped box on the left has a hinged top. The maple-leaf-shaped box in the middle has a removable top. (See Illus. 11-10.) Glue the bottom of the shell-shaped box to the rest of the box after cutting the inside out. Cut the bottom of the leaf-shaped box off the inside waste, and glue it to the inside of the box. By gluing the bottom to the inside of the box, you ensure that there is no seam on the outside of the box. I used a gap-filling glue from Garrett Wade to glue the bottom in place. Cover the inside of the box with spray-on suede.

The box shown in Illus. 11-11 is made with a series of cuts. Do the following:

1. Cut the bottom off.

2. Cut out the key shown on the left in Illus. 11-11.

3. Cut the top off.

4. Cut a hole out of the middle.

5. Glue the bottom in place again. Cover the inside with spray-on suede.

These three examples show the basic design options for box construction. You can use almost any pattern for the outside shape of the box. Experiment with this process on scrap wood before you start using good wood.

Illus. 11-9. *These three boxes were made with a band saw.*

Illus. 11-10. *The box on the left has a hinged lid. The box on the right has a removable lid.*

Illus. 11-11. *The key on the left must be pulled out before the lid will slide out.*

Making Containers

Using a technique similar to that used to make decorative boxes, it is possible to make containers for a variety of objects. The bird and the pig shown in Illus. 11-12 are hollow inside, like the boxes. The bird holds postage stamps. The pig functions as a piggy bank. To make the bird and pig, do the following:

1. Cut the inside out, leaving an opening for the stamps or coins.

2. Glue the sides to the middle piece. This forms the container.

Intarsia

Intarsia is a technique in which solid wood is cut and fitted together, forming a design. (See Illus. 11-13.) To use this technique, do the following:

1. Hold the curved piece momentarily on top of the neighboring piece, and trace the outline with a pencil.

2. Use a narrow blade to cut next to the pencil line.

3. Sand the pieces.

4. Glue the pieces together.

Illus. 11-12. *The bird container on the left holds stamps. On the right is a piggy bank.*

Illus. 11-13. *This box was made by Barbara Reifschneider of Colchester, CT. She used the technique of intarsia to make it.*

Tilted-Table Techniques

You can achieve interesting results by tilting the table and making internal cuts on the workpiece. The saw blade removes material from the kerf, leaving a space between the two pieces.

When you make an internal cut, cut on an angle. The inside piece will slide into the piece that it was cut from. (See Illus. 11-14.)

Table-tilting techniques can be used to make different designs or to provide a practical function. Illus. 11-15 shows how tilting the table can affect the design of scroll-saw letters. This technique was also used to make the fold-down baskets shown in Illus. 11-16.

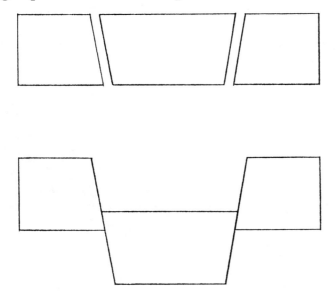

Illus. 11-14. *Two pieces will fit tightly together if you cut tight curves and tilt the table.*

Table 2. *This chart gives the table tilt angle for different thicknesses of wood. It was created by Beau Lowerr and first published in a Wisconsin Woodworkers Guild 1988 newsletter.*

		"BACKGROUND" WOOD THICKNESS				
		0.125	0.250	0.375	0.500	0.750
		DEGREES TABLE TILT FROM HORIZONTAL				
S	0.015	6.9	3.4			
A	0.016	7.4	3.7			
W	0.017	7.8	3.9			
	0.018	8.3	4.1			
K	0.019	8.7	4.4	2.9		
E	0.020		4.6	3.1		
R	0.021		4.8	3.2		
F	0.022		5.0	3.4		
	0.023		5.3	3.5		
	0.024		5.5	3.7		
	0.025		5.7	3.8	2.9	1.9
	0.026			4.0	3.0	2.0
	0.027			4.1	3.1	2.1
	0.028			4.3	3.2	2.1
	0.029			4.4	3.3	2.2
	0.030			4.6	3.4	2.3

Illus. 11-15. *These letters were cut with the table tilted.*

Illus. 11-16. *These folding baskets were cut with the table tilted at 5½ degrees.*

Lamination

When narrow strips of wood are glued together in a bent form, the resulting piece retains the shape of the form after the glue dries. Lamination is extremely strong and is cost-effective, in that a lot of material does not have to be cut away to form a curved shape. The only waste is the kerf that is cut between the individual pieces.

Illus. 11-17 shows a laminated shelf bracket and a lamination form for creating a gentle curve. The glued-laminated strips are covered with wax paper so that the piece doesn't become attached to the form. Illus. 11-18 shows a glue-laminated curved bed. The plate shown in Illus. 11-19, made by a retired music teacher, is made of scrap wood that was cut narrow and laminated.

Most laminations can be glued together after being cut on a band saw. No sanding or planing is needed.

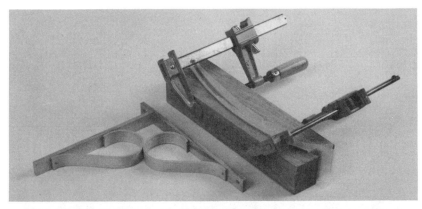

Illus. 11-17. At left is a laminated shelf bracket, and at right a typical lamination form. The wax paper prevents the glued piece from sticking to the form.

Illus. 11-18. This bed was designed and made by Jeff Miller of Chicago. The front and back curves are laminated. (Photo courtesy of Jeff Miller)

Illus. 11-19. This laminated plate is made from scrap wood. The pieces were glued in a form with a slight curve.

Kerfing

Kerfing is a technique used to curve wood. Kerfing is done by making a series of incomplete crosscuts. (See Illus. 11-20.) About ¹⁄₁₆ inch of wood remains. This wood has the flexible characteristics of veneer, which allows the piece to bend in either direction. If you glue a piece of veneer to the kerfed side, the dried piece will hold the desired curve and will be very strong. (See Illus. 11-21.) The piece will be even stronger if you fill the kerfs with a gap-filling glue. Kerfing is a very useful technique to use for making curves that will not show on the finished project,

such as lamination forms or pieces of furniture where the side shows but not the edge.

The crosscuts are usually spaced about ¹⁄₈ inch from each other. You may want to experiment to see how widely to space the cuts for your particular application. The wider the kerf and the closer the cuts, the tighter the turn.

You can also glue canvas to the wood and make the kerf cuts. This makes the resulting piece even more flexible, without the potential for breakage. You can also glue canvas between two pieces of wood, and then make the kerf cuts. This makes the piece very flexible in both directions. This technique was used to make the toy dinosaur shown in Illus. 11-22.

Illus. 11-20. *Kerfing is done by making a series of incomplete crosscuts.*

Illus. 11-21. *When a piece of veneer is glued to the kerfed side, the piece maintains the curve of the bending form.*

Illus. 11-22. *This toy dinosaur has a piece of canvas glued between the kerfed boards. See page 126 for the pattern for this toy.*

Interior Cuts

Although the band-saw blade cannot be taken apart and reattached inside a hole, it can make interior cuts if you use the cut and glue technique described in Chapter 7. Another way to make interior cuts is to make a saw cut into the waste area, and then remove the waste. (See Illus. 11-23.) After removing the waste, glue the opening back together. (See Illus. 11-24.) Gluing the piece back together is effective if the piece is flexible and the slight bending will not cause it to break. However, if you are afraid that bending the piece together at the glue joint will cause a break, glue a small piece of wood, such as veneer, into the seam.

Keep the outside area square until the glue dries. This gives you a place to apply pressure with the clamp. After the piece is dry, finish the outside cut.

Illus. 11-23. *Make a straight cut into the interior and remove the waste.*

Illus. 11-24. *Then glue the kerf back together. Keep the outside square until the glue dries. When the glue is dry, finish the outside.*

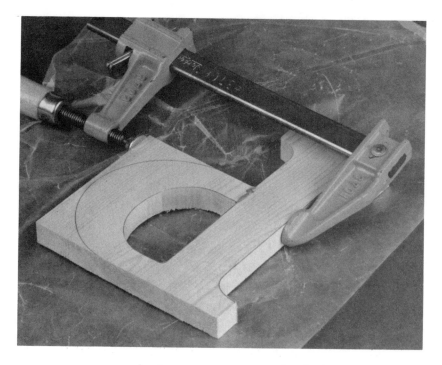

Sanding

About the only disadvantage to using the band saw is that the surface of the cut is not perfectly smooth. A jointer or planer can be used to smooth broad surfaces, but on curves sanding is the best choice.

Some band saws have an optional sanding belt and platen to support the belt. Narrow belt sanders are also available, and save the time and effort needed to change belts. These belt sanders can be fitted with a half-inch belt. (See Illus. 11-25.) The narrow belt is useful for sanding patterns with multiple curves. (See Illus. 11-26.)

When using the belt sander or the sanding attachment, it is very important that the belt and the table be square. This should be checked

Illus. 11-25. *The narrow belt sander is useful for smoothing a sawed surface.*

Illus. 11-26. *The curves in this toy were sanded with a ½-inch belt sander.*

often. (See Illus. 11-27.) Use a try square to check that they are square.

The disc sander is useful for sanding work that is either flat or convex (hollowed or rounded outward). (See Illus. 11-28 and 11-29.) Use the area as close to the outside of the disc as possible. Once again, it is very important that the table and the sanding surface be square.

For interior or concave areas, a sanding drum works well. There are kits available that have a number of different-sized drums. (See Illus. 11-30.) These drums are usually used with a drill press, but can also be used with a hand-held drill.

Bigger sanding drums are available that can be used to sand large concave areas. Illus. 11-31 shows the types of drum that are available. The smaller drum, on the left, can be inflated with a bike-tire pump. The larger drum, on the right, is filled with foam rubber. The sanding belt is pressure-fitted onto it, and is held in place by centrifugal force.

Illus. 11-27. *Check often to make sure that the belt is square to the table.*

Illus. 11-28. *The disc sander is used to smooth convex surfaces.*

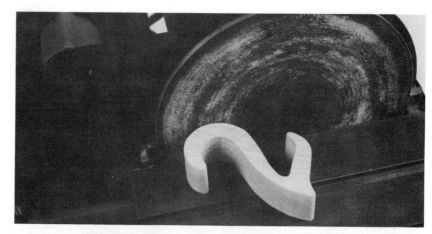

Illus. 11-29. *The disc sander can also be used to sand a flat surface. Try to match the grain of the wood with the direction the disc rotates at.*

Illus. 11-30. *Small sanding drums work well in small concave areas. The small drums are usually available in a set.*

Illus. 11-31. *The sanding drum on the left is inflatable. The drum on the right is made of foam. These drums are useful for sanding large concave areas.*

Chapter 12

PROJECTS

This last chapter includes patterns and instructions for simple projects that can be made with a band saw. As a beginner, you may discover that you will not get totally satisfying results the first time you try to make these projects. Do not become frustrated. Just remember that the band saw takes patience and practice. If things do not go well the first time, just try again. Don't be too goal-oriented. Experimenting with the band saw is the key to achieving success and skill.

When you feel that you are ready for more information concerning the band saw, I suggest that you acquire my other book, *Band Saw Handbook*, which is also published by Sterling Publishing Company. That book contains information on more advanced cutting techniques, presents more extensive guidelines on tuning, adjustment, and maintenance, and provides an array of challenging projects.

Pine and Redwood Car

The pine and redwood car shown in Illus. 12-1 and 12-2 is a simple project to make. Since the two fenders are identical, you can cut them at the same time. Use double-face tape or hot-melt glue to hold the fenders together during the sawing and the sanding processes. The wheels can be cut on the band saw, or they can be purchased from a local supplier or a woodworking catalogue. The technique for cutting a circle on the band saw is described in Chapter 9.

Cut the fenders and the body out and sand them. Drill the holes and then glue the fenders to the body. Mount the wheels last.

Illus. 12-1. *This car is made of pine. The darker fenders are made of redwood.*

Illus. 12-2. Pattern for the car. Each square in this pattern equals ¾ inch.

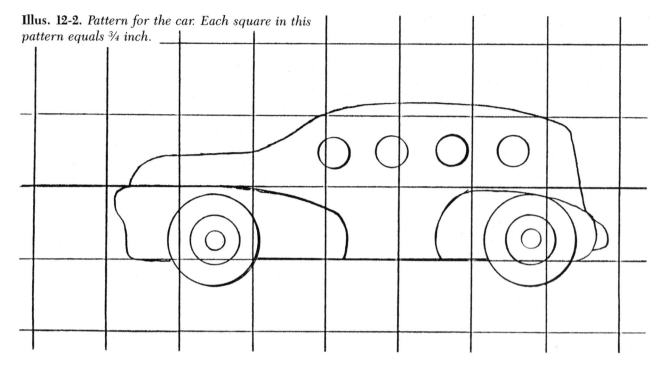

Snowflake

The snowflake shown in Illus. 12-3 and 12-4 is made of thin plywood. Plywood is stronger than solid wood, but the real advantage is that plywood does not break when it is cut into small, delicate pieces. The plywood for this project is ¼ inch thick. This type of wood is available at wood and hobby shops and can also be ordered by mail.

This snowflake can be made a number of dif- ferent ways. One technique is to make two complete snowflakes, cut one in half, and glue the two halves to the other snowflake. If you are going to make two snowflakes, it makes sense to cut both at the same time. The two pieces of wood can be cut at the same time if they are glued or taped together.

Another option, which is faster, is to cut a number of sections of the snowflake at one time and then to glue them together. This is called stack sawing and is described in detail in Chapter 11.

Illus. 12-3. The stack-sawing technique for cutting this snowflake is described in Chapter 11.

Illus. 12-4. *Pattern for the snowflake. This pattern is full-size. Use the triangle shape on top if you are going to stack-saw 12 pieces at one time. This technique is shown on page 106.*

Bird Stamp Holder

The stamp holder in the shape of a bird, shown in Illus. 12-5 and 12-6, is made of three pieces—a middle piece and two sides. There are two openings. The large opening is for inserting the roll of stamps. The small opening, or mouth, is the exit for the individual stamps.

The best blade to use to make this project is a ⅛-inch-wide blade with a pitch of 14 TPI. It is best to cut the outside of the three pieces at the same time. After cutting the outside, cut out the inside of the middle piece. Make the saw cut at the mouth last.

Because the breast of the bird is loose, you should tape it to the larger middle piece before gluing the sides. Use toothpicks to keep the mouth open. Run the tape all the way around the middle piece so that the breast is held secure.

Illus. 12-5. *Bird stamp holder.*

Illus. 12-6. *Full-size pattern for the bird stamp holder.*

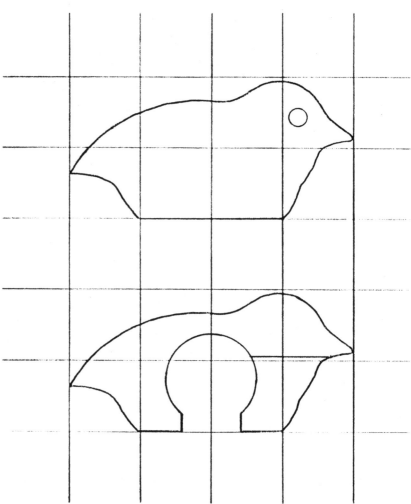

Cut and Glue Projects

The cut and glue technique is used for making interior cuts with the band saw. The interior cuts can be either decorative or functional. The pencil holder and deer mirror presented here and on pages 122–125 employ the cut and glue technique. You may want to review the technique in Chapter 7 before you start.

Pencil Holder

The two matching halves which create the pencil holder are actually a decoration about ¼ inch thick that is glued to the front of a solid block that is 2 inches thick. After the glue has dried, drill the holes that accept the pencils. Next, round the corners. Use the band saw to remove the waste. Last, use a router with a roundover bit to create a radius on the edge of the top and the holes.

Illus. 12-7. *Pencil holder.*

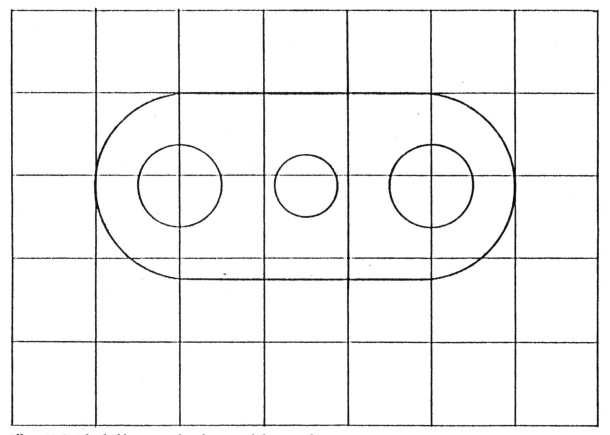

Illus. 12-8. *The half-pattern for the top of the pencil holder. The wood used is 2¼ inches thick.*

Illus. 12-9. *The front pattern for the pencil holder. This is also a half pattern.*

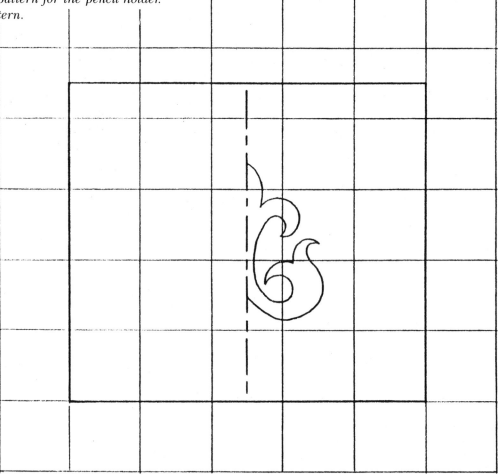

Deer Mirror

In this project, the two halves of the door are not the same, and thus cannot be cut at the same time. Also, this mirror is more complicated to make because the inside piece tapers from front to back and is actually wedged and glued in the outside piece.

The mirror is not hard to make if you follow the correct sequence of procedures. Do the following:

1. Clamp the two boards together.

2. Attach the pattern to the two boards with rubber cement.

3. Remove the clamps and separate the two pieces by cutting the paper pattern with an Exacto knife.

4. Make the inside and outside cuts with the table 90 degrees to the blade.

5. Make the middle cut with the table tilted 5 degrees to the blade.

6. Glue the two pieces together using large rubber bands as clamps.

7. Sand the surfaces of the inside rim and outside rim carefully.

8. Fit the inside rim to the outside rim.

9. After the two pieces are fitted together, apply the glue carefully.

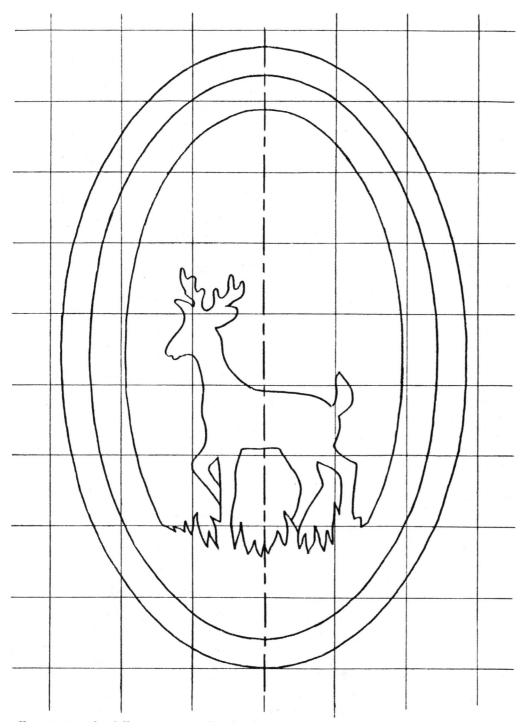

Illus. 12-10. *The full-size pattern for the deer mirror. Make the middle cut with the table tilted at a 5-degree angle.*

Illus. 12-11. *A deer mirror made of walnut. To make this mirror, cut the outside rim with the table tilted 5 degrees to the blade, push the middle forward, and then glue it in place.*

Early American Mirror

Illus. 12-12. *A small, early American mirror.*

Illus. 12-13. *The full-size pattern for the small mirror. The bottom of the mirror is made from a moulding that is 6 inches wide and 8 inches long.*

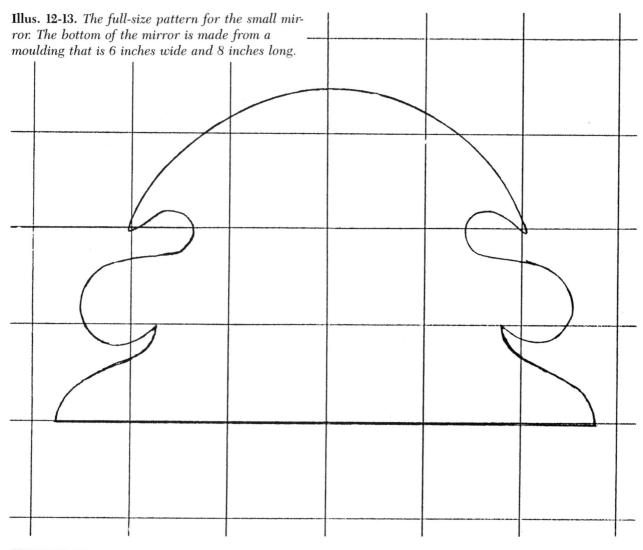

Toy Dinosaur

Illus. 12-14. *This toy dinosaur is made with the kerfing technique. Cloth or canvas is glued between the two pieces of wood. Kerfing is described in Chapter 11. See the following page for the pattern.*

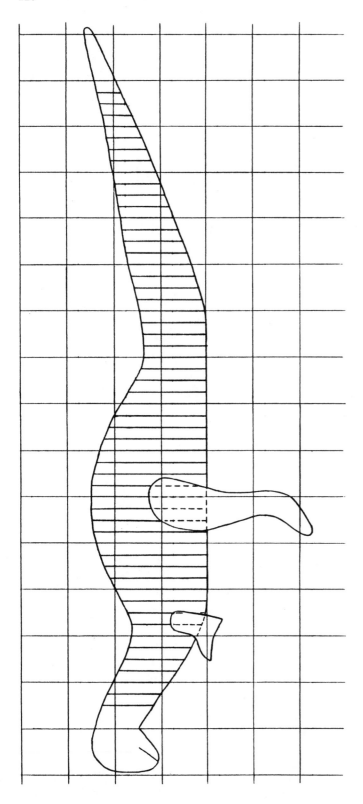

Illus. 12-15. *The pattern for the toy dinosaur. Each square is equal to 1 inch.*

Index

Making Wood Boxes with a Band Saw

Explores ways to use ordinary scrap wood or pieces of plywood, pine, poplar, or cedar to make over 30 spectacular boxes. Step-by-step construction tips, patterns, drawings, and photos show how to make marbleized jewelry boxes, hinged, loose-lid and flip-top boxes, and boxes in the shape of ducks, turtles, and crocodiles, and more.

Band Saw Handbook

A comprehensive look at the popular power tool that explores the different types of saws and blades available, how to adjust and tune the band saw, the complete range of basic and advanced cutting techniques, and much more. Also includes a project section.

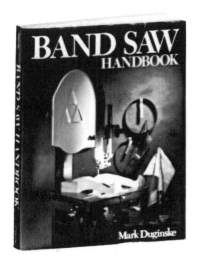

Band Saw Projects

Provides patterns, photos, and instructions for making over 20 projects from vases and jewelry boxes to wind chimes. This guide book also explains techniques such as scaling patterns with a pantograph, constructing an ovaler to make perfect ovals, creating handsome contrasts with different woods and stains, and much more.